Places You Want To Go

Places You Want To Go

William Guest

Copyright © 2016 William Guest
All Rights Reserved

ISBN: 978-1-942956-29-7
Library of Congress Control Number: 2016943909

Manufactured in the United States

Lamar University Literary Press
Beaumont, Texas

For

Amy, my late wife, my companion on the Arctic trip

Floyd, my brother, my companion on the Antarctic trip

Maureen Odriscoll-Levy, M.D., my companion on the Sligo, Ireland trip

Recent Nonfiction from Lamar University Press

Jean Andrews, *High Tides, Low Tides*
Robert Murray Davis, *Levels of Incompetence: An Academic Life*
Ted L. Estess, *Fishing Spirit Lake*
Dominique Inge, *A Garden on the Brazos*
Jim McJunkin, *Deep Sleep*
Jeanetta Calhoun Mish, *Oklahomeland*
Jim Sanderson, *Sanderson's Fiction Writing Manual*
Steven Schroeder, *What's Love Got to Do With It? A city out of thin air*

For Information on these and other books, go to
www.lamar.edu/literarypress

Acknowledgments

I cannot count all of the people who have somehow enhanced my interest in geography, exploration and language, there have been so many, in varied ways. Accounts of the many daunting explorers whose names often adorn the earth's exotic regions, the grand and romantic expeditions, the wonders of this earth, how we have only recently achieved its outer boundaries. The artists who have depicted its grandeur on canvas and in words—prose and poetry. Expressions of exuberance and love that we have for its abundance, beauty, generous support for our lives, its comparisons to other bodies in our universe, and the huge and varied animal life that are companions in our travels and existence.

If only I could have had the perch to look at this earth from outer space, I would have tipped my hat to it and all that mankind has done and experienced on it.

Books from Lamar University Press

Jean Andrews, *High Tides, Low Tides: the Story of Leroy Colombo*
Charles Behlen, *Failing Heaven*
Alan Berecka, *With Our Baggage*
David Bowles, *Flower, Song, Dance: Aztec and Mayan Poetry*
Jerry Bradley, *Crownfeathers and Effigies*
Terry Dalrymple, *Love Stories, Sort Of*
Chip Dameron, *Waiting for an Etcher*
Robert Murray Davis, *Levels of Incompetence: An Academic Life*
William Virgil Davis, *The Bones Poems*
Jeffrey Delotto, *Voices Writ in Sand*
Gerald Duff, *Memphis Mojo*
Ted L. Estess, *Fishing Spirit Lake*
Mimi Ferebee, *Wildfires and Atmospheric Memories*
Ken Hada, *Margaritas and Redfish*
Michelle Hartman, *Disenchanted and Disgruntled*
Michelle Hartman, *Irony and Irreverence*
Katherine Hoerth, *Goddess Wears Cowboy Boots*
Lynn Hoggard, *Motherland, Stories and Poems from Louisiana*
Dominique Inge, *A Garden on the Brazos*
Gretchen Johnson, *The Joy of Deception*
Gretchen Johnson, *A Trip Through Downer, Minnesota*
Laozi, *the daodejing*, tr. David Breeden, Steven Schroeder, Wally Swist
Christopher Linforth, *When You Find Us We Will Be Gone*
Tom Mack and Andrew Geyer, editors, *A Shared Voice*
Dave Oliphant, *The Pilgrimage, Selected Poems: 1962-2012*
Janet McCann, *The Crone at the Casino*
Erin Murphy, *Ancilla*
Kornelijus Platelis, *Solitary Architectures*
Harold Raley, *Louisiana Rogue*
Carol Coffee Reposa, *Underground Musicians*
Carol Smallwood, *Water, Earth, Air, Fire, and Picket Fences*
Jim Sanderson, *Trashy Behavior*
Jim Sanderson, *Sanderson's Fiction Writing Manual*
Jan Seale, *Appearances*
Jan Seale, *The Parkinson Poems*
Melvin Sterne, *The Number You Have Reached*
John Wegner, *Love is Not a Dirty Word and Other Stories*
Robert Wexelblatt, *The Artist Wears Rough Clothing*
Jonas Zdanys, *Pushing the Envelope*

For more information about these and other books, go to
www.lamar.edu/literarypress

CONTENTS

11   Introduction

13   Preface: Antarctic

44   Arctic

59   Peru, Amazon, Cusco

110   Yeats Poetry Festival: Sligo, Ireland

135   Notes

Introduction

I have been fortunate. In our time, travel is easy. Many destinations, many opportunities. Dreams and curiosities can be pursued. Expanding knowledge of who we are and where we live. This earth is no longer that huge, partially explored, bi-polar, rotating round ball that it always was until the recent past that's now fading behind us, rapidly it seems. Now all of its places have been found and described, at least in the large picture.

But each one of us has places we have not seen that we want to see. There are places that call to us. Places we want to go. When I went to Antarctica (the first trip reflected in these journals), I had already lived a long life, traveled a lot to Europe, Canada, Mexico. But in the travel-lust background of my mind I nurtured a few places that also had the whiff of adventure and wonderment, in large part because of reading the stories as I was growing up. About Antarctica, the Arctic, the Amazon. Places I wanted to see, that had about them an aura of grandness, magnetism. One of these journals goes to Sligo, Ireland, for a Yeats Poetry Festival. I have a love affair with Ireland, and have been there many times.

I had to slot the time, allot the funds, make the plans, and go. The journals presented here were written in each case within the experience of the trip, finding time to write, moving on when perhaps my information was sketchy, even with mistakes unknown at the time, but having the juice of freshness and excitement. The Arctic journal is the only exception, written upon returning home, but still some freshness. In each case the photos were added upon returning home, and a few organizing issues resolved, but I avoided correcting and rewriting, and what you read is the way it was written inside the experience, the way it was minted.

There was no plan to publish them, although I did post them on my website. The publisher serendipitously saw them on my website and invited me to publish, which I gladly accepted. Each journal will contain information about why I wanted to make that particular trip, and will have information about their being written contemporaneously, even though I have repeated it here.

Also, as another in-part repetition, there are important issues and changes occurring for these places that are not addressed in the journals. Antarctica and the Arctic are much in the news because of global warming, and the prospect that it may become severe. The impact of this on animal life threatens to be dire, and we see signs already. One small modification: we did have on the Antarctica trip a film and discussion of line fishing and its tragic consequences for sea birds. Generally our focus, and my focus, was to see what was there to see, and to talk about what we're seeing, and some history. Activities, thus focused, filled our agenda, even though we were aware of the background noise of what's happening to our earth.

Each journey is quite different from the others, in two cases: poles apart. If I have anything to offer, it is the freshness of the eye of a non-professional happy, eager adventurer. And hope that the writing will help you enjoy.

If you have not been there, maybe you will want to go.

Preface: Antarctic

A journal to capture a trip to the southern end of the earth, complete with astonishing geology, scenery and animals. What to put in; what to leave out? This preface is needed only to help identify some boundaries affecting this account. One guiding principle was to move right along, with the result that explanations and "background" had to be sacrificed. Another objective was to maintain the language as it was originally penned, on the trip, and not to edit it into a more finished product. This increased the risk of mistakes in order to preserve the "contemporaneous" aspect. This preface is written "after"; the journal was written "during."

Here is some preface information. My brother, Floyd, made the trip with me. The trip was with a group on a cruise ship, sailing from the southern tip of Tierra del Fuego (which is at the southern tip of South America) across the Drake Passage to the Peninsular of Antarctica (after first spending 3 days in Santiago, Chile, where the cruse members assembled). The continent of Antarctica is huge, 90% covered with ice. Its rainfall is comparable to the Sahara Desert, so the abundant ice and snow is the result of accumulations over millions of years. It is home of some 75% of the earth's fresh water, locked up in ice. It is surrounded by the Southern Ocean. It doubles in size from summer (November—March) to winter. The ice shelves that occur in various edges of the continent expand in winter. Does seawater freeze? Yes, but in doing so, beginning a couple of degrees below the freezing temperature for fresh water, one of nature's miracles in converting seawater to ice is to squeeze out a large amount of the salt. It has the coldest temperatures on earth, and the fiercest, most stormy winds. Even in the summer much of the continent is not readily accessible.

This trip (a typical one), requiring 2½ days to cross the Drake, was to spend 5 days on the Peninsular which extends in a long curved "narrow" stretch of land northward toward the southern tip of Chile/Argentina (both countries share the southernmost South America land and islands). One of the rare islands to encounter "on the way" across the Drake is Elephant Island. A thick chain of islands hugs the west side of the Peninsular, relatively near the continent. The landings were mostly on some of these islands, with one landing on the continent itself. (A "landing" is a transfer by a zodiac boat from ship to shore, as there are no facilities for ships to dock.) Ice at Hope Bay prevented a planned entrance there. The southernmost reach of the trip was slightly less than one degree of latitude short of the Antarctic Circle (66 degrees, 33 minutes, south latitude), which may have been because of the amount of ice in the proximity of the Circle. So, the "trip to Antarctica" was to a small patch of Antarctica, considering the huge size of "Antarctica," consisting only of "touching" the northwestern extension of the Peninsular and coastal islands. (One accepted definition of "Antarctica" is: that area south of 60 degrees south latitude.)

However, this was a lot. Animals were in abundance. The southern ocean and environs comprise an extremely rich feeding area for whales, seals, penguins, birds and other animals. The extremely cold water from the icy continent encounters the warmer Pacific and Atlantic waters, churning up low-level nutrients, feeding the growth of krill and shrimp, and so on up the food chain. The continent, some 180 million years ago, was known as Gondwana and through the process of plate tectonics divided into South

American, Africa, India, Australia, New Zealand and, of course, Antarctica. The drama of the landscapes resulting from the geological dynamics is astounding. And the roughness of the oceans, the grand scale of ice formations exhibited in so many ways, and the animals: some whale sightings, birds, birds, birds, seals, seals, seals and penguins, penguins, penguins, penguins. There's so much.

Topics such as global warming, the breaking up of the ice shelves, environmental concerns, political interests, and scientific research are very important but not the focus of this trip. What I saw is what you get.

ANTARTIC

December 28, 2003

On the plane somewhere over Chile. En route to Santiago, from Houston by way of Dallas. Using a flashlight in the darkened plane. This is written at 4:30 a.m. (Houston time) and the light has begun to appear from shuttered windows. About 3 hours to arrival. (Santiago is 2 time-zones to the east of Houston, but 3 hours time difference because Chile is on daylight savings time and Houston is currently not.) Breakfast in about one hour, wishfully. My brother, Floyd, is 2 seats over (vacant seat between us). Seems to be asleep, although aisle traffic is stirring as passengers begin to wake.

So this begins a journal of my trip to Antarctica. First, 3 days in Santiago. On the third day after arrival in Santiago, December 31, 2003, the expedition passengers will gather at the Hyatt Regency Hotel —alumni of Yale and Harvard, about 107 strong. On January 1, a charter flight to Ushuaia, Argentina, at the Tierra del Fuego tip of South America. Board The Orion. Sail across the Drake Passage to the Antarctica Peninsular. But this is getting ahead.

I have wanted to make this trip for a number of years. Why? I have continued to ask myself that question. The night before leaving, a woman at a dinner party asked me that question (the only person to have done so). I replied: I think that this trip will help to fill in the picture that I am so curious about regarding our planet earth—its extensiveness, diversity, history, plasticity—the sense that the planet is like a living thing, changing over great time spans that are difficult to grasp. It's not easy to construct the big picture over long, long time.

This topic was developed in our conversation. So, as I think about why I want to go to Antarctica, I now believe that my reply was the basic answer. Sailing across the Drake Passage, seeing the ice and snow, the grandness of the geography and geology, the abundant and extraordinary wildlife adapted to harsh conditions, garnering a sense of place on the globe, reading and hearing about the Antarctica explorers whose names adorn the region's map, and slotting these activities into the timeline of the earth and man-on-earth adventures that they pursued at this place. This is what I expect to experience and this is what draws me to Antarctica.

Breakfast arrived.

A little later, after breakfast and filing out the arrival forms (announcement that we are 200 miles from Santiago), I moved to an area to view through a window: I saw the Andes! Great folds of mountainous region, mist and black and gray and snow-pockets strewed together, as the sunlight heralded another day across the long, peak-studded sweep of the famous and great Andes Mountains. Out of the plane's left windows are the Andes. To the right, the great Pacific, named by Magellan (maybe?) in 1519 when he heroically sailed through the straits bearing his name at the end of the South American continent, threading through the southern archipelago of islands that marks the termination of the South American continent and the beginning of the region of ocean where the Atlantic and Pacific meet in a stretch across some 600 miles to the Southern Ocean and Antarctica, named the Drake Passage. On Magellan's left as he discovered the much-sought-after passageway was a large stretch of land, now known to be a very large island, where he saw fires continuously burning but knew not the reason, and he called the place Tierra del Fuego.

December 29, 2003

Today our guide, German (not a German name, but the name "German") met us at the airport, took us to the Hyatt at 11 a.m., then picked us up at 1 p.m. for a tour of the Maipo Canyon region, southeast of Santiago (toward the mountains), including a 1-hour tour of the Concha y Toro Winery—one of the worlds' largest, with beautiful grounds and a long history.

We had arrived at the airport at about 10 a.m., a little late. Paid $100 entry fee, then passed through customs, etc., and met German who was waiting for us. Officials processing us through were amazingly cold and distant, but, maybe it doesn't matter and just the nature of customs processing. (Later experiences were that Chilean people were quite warm and friendly.)

German was warm and service oriented, a really accommodating person—
about 62 years old (seemed younger), 2 children (son and daughter, 37 and 39) and 4 grandchildren. Has traveled some (France, Spain, Austria and maybe other places), years ago when a young man (at age 20, hitchhiked all the way from Santiago to New York, where he met his wife-to-be, a Chilean native working at the glove counter at Saks). Very good communicator about Chile, the region, history, etc., and not intrusive.

A long drive from the Hyatt to get out of town. German said that it's about 20 miles (30 kilometers, roughly) from the center of town in any direction to get out of the city. The road began to rise out of Santiago into the Maipo Canyon region, and we arrived soon to a 2:30 winery tour. The tour was typical winery talk, madepleasant by a bright young witty man. About the establishment, the statistics, production and market coverage (which is huge), the founding, the family, etc. Three tastings: Chardonnay, Merlot and Cabinet Sauvignon—all quite ordinary to my taste.

On to the uplands, to see the Maipo River and related landscape. Great rises of mountains in the back range—weekend getaway, residences of considerable substance, as well as more modest weekend inns and residences. We visited a French restaurant in which the owner invested
a lot of money, construction, panache, dreams, idiosyncrasies and pride. Had a beer, looked at the menu (which looked really good), took some pictures and headed for Santiago, down the river valley.

German took us to the central city area. Floyd and I walked along the pedestrian malls (cars not allowed, and paved for pedestrian-walking), seeing Constitution Square and other landmark sites. Street entertainers were busy—like you often see in New Orleans. Crowded shops of jewelry, cameras, shoes, etc. and much etc.—none of which seemed to matter but it was dense and stretched on for blocks and blocks. Galleria galore. Crowded streets and sidewalks, like New York. It's curious to see Christmas decorations, and hear, to some extent, Christmas music, even when it feels like, and is, summertime. The city has 6.5 million people.

Dinner at a "regional" restaurant suggested by German (who took us to it and helped us settle in to the table, menu, waiter, and specials of the house). We had a delightful bottle of Chardonnay, seafood platter appetizer (a variety of at least 10 kinds of seafood). I had a fish soup—very good, filled with several kinds of sea-things. Floyd had an abalone pie (but we couldn't figure out why the word "pie")— it was a nicely presented abalone. Interesting sauces on the side.

German, who had waited in the car for us, took us back to the hotel and we, exhausted, to bed at 10:30.

Tuesday, December 30

Breakfast at Hyatt's swell restaurant. Lots of pleasant waiters (wait persons), with "chefs" at the buffet to prepare omelets or whatever. To the room, ironed 2 shirts (washed the night before) and hurriedly met German (6 minutes late) for the 9 a.m. pick-up.

Driving southwest for miles and miles (actually, kilometers and kilometers in Chile), through a very fertile valley of vegetables, fruit trees, vineyards, country scenes—very beautiful land, and well maintained and husbanded. (To the southwest is headed toward the coast. The day before was southeast into the mountains.) The day's trip pointed to San Antonio, a port city (one of 2 major ports "serving" Santiago and region—and there are many in Chile, with 2300 miles of coastline), Isla Negro (one of the homes of Pablo Neruda, Nobel poet laureate, 1904-1973), Casablanca, Vena del Mar, Valparaiso (Chile's 2nd largest city) and will be back in Santiago by 7 p.m.

Views. The coast is miles and miles like the coastlines of Oregon, Cote d'azur and Costa Brava. Sea lions lounging on rock outcroppings just off shore, pelicans on rock ledges, beautiful beaches, waves of the whitest foams constantly splashing upon the rocks or curving along the beach shoreline. The land allows room for roads and beaches along the shore, but then climbs up steep mountain sides thoroughly covered with apartments, homes, high rises, hotels, etc. etc. And this is mile after mile, with occasional land-inlets for a small village or government buildings (such as the Naval Academy of Armaments).

Pablo Neruda's house. Did you think I would pass by without speaking of it? It is awesome. I tried to think of a way to describe how I felt much of the time as our guide (Doris, a lovely American woman) led us from room to room. I thought: like the feeling that comes with a sudden gasp of breath much needed. A feeling of glad fullness, a viscerally tight happy inside. Doris talked warmly of his life, telling about his 3 wives, the death of his child Malva Marina at age 8 from hydrocephalus. (She said "water on the brain"—when we know that many years later a surgical procedure was developed to treat the condition.)

What a collection of eclectic interests, an artist's eye and taste, a child-like enjoyment, eccentric and outlandish: sculpted prows of sailing ships (bowsprit figureheads) (7 or 10 or so throughout), colored glass, masks from several cultures (really excellent specimen), ship models, ships in bottles, sea shells, hats, life-size horse of wood and papier mache (that stood outside a store until the owner finally agreed to sell it to Neruda after 40 years of negotiation), furniture designed by Neruda, 2 outstanding fireplaces, rooms (all small but exactly right) with fabulous views, interesting passages and construction materials (one entrance floor of black "concrete" with embedded seashells), and on and on. Books and books, of course. I cannot believe that one man with only one life could "collect" so much and so well. And Doris pointed out that Neruda had 2 other houses—one in Santiago and one in Valparaiso. (We will see the

Santiago house tomorrow but did not have time in Valparaiso to capture the 3rd).

The view: Perched on top of a cliff-rise above a small beach enclave and beautiful black rock-laced sand-shore, its rooms serve several scene-directions. The sea constantly inundates its splashing against the rocks and beaches, along in's and out's of an irregular cliff-based shoreline, spreading white water-spray that continuously unveils appearances and disappearances, like nature playing with smoke and mirrors to keep you mesmerized.

The political aspects. Neruda served in diplomatic posts: Java, Spain (where he became a Communist), France (and other places?). Political and publicly active, he was in favor with earlier governments and Allente but not with Panochet whose government menaced the Isla Negra house and only miraculously were the contents not confiscated. He died of cancer at age 69 in 1973 during Pinochet's rule. I am somewhat acquainted, over the years, with Neruda's poetry, and it is good. Also I've seen "The Postman" (the Italian movie with Neruda prominently in the story line). Now I will re-visit his poetry with a much better sense of the person and his setting. I wonder sometimes if this does, or does not, matter when reading poetry.

This was a moving treat, then on to Vena del Mar and lunch at 2:30 at Edelweiss at Vena del Mar, pre-arranged fare of pisco sour (a special Chilean drink reminiscent of margaritas, but very smooth, a little fruity, probably strong medicine, but delicious), shrimp appetizer with Chardonnay, salmon topped with spinach puree and crème boulee with espresso (2) to complete it. The view was astonishingly beautiful.

The day continued in rich mountains-come-down-to-the-sea geological drama, all day long.

About 5 p.m., headed back to Santiago along a different route but through similar lush valley farmland. It does not freeze in this valley, although this is only about 100 kilometers from the steep rise of mountains that are covered in snow for several winter months.

In town we stopped for cheese and bread. Floyd had bought a bottle of Merlot at Concha y Toro the day before. At the hotel (8 p.m.) we went to the exercise room for some very welcome exercise, and took a swim in the capacious pool nestled in the beautiful grounds. The water was like ice water, but, as Floyd remarked, we are in Chile.

In the room, no corkscrew, but housekeeping to the rescue. Bread, cheese, wine, looking north through a large room-length window to the Andes mountains, while light was fading slowly down at about 9:30. What a day! What a view! Then this writing with the pleasure, like playing back a video of the day in my head.

Wednesday, December 31, 2003

Today, 10 a.m., started the city tour. Much traffic during the day because businesses closed at various mid-day hours and frustrated us by finding a few of our intended sites closed (the Palacio Cousino, the funicular). We had planned a trip up the mountain on the funicular, then across to the next mountain on the cable car for views.

We did get to the Neruda house—his Santiago house at the end of the street. Located there because it began as a "tryst" house with Matilda, his Chilean mistress/lover who later became his third and last wife. The house's location was to have privacy and secrecy, as he was still married to his Argentine wife (20 years older) whom he later "left." (Divorce is not allowed in Chile but somehow things are worked out. In fact, as I write there is an upcoming moment [election, parliament ?] for approving, or disapproving, the granting of divorces, which is likely to fail, according to German, because Chile is 70% Catholic.)

Anyway, Neruda and Matilda finally worked it out, later bought the house and made changes and collections. (The Isla Negra house later became an additional seaside house.) The tour of the house was like the Isla Negra house in many ways—about Neruda, Matilda, houses, life of Neruda, collections, his writing and diplomatic life, etc. The Santiago house is likewise amazing. Neruda's house furnishings are eclectic in the delightful extreme—vibrantly and intensively eclectic. Nothing whatever is wasted. Each and every piece of the objects-packed house is a twist or a turn or an art object or a clever idea of a personal imprint. The lamps are—several of them—ship lamps. There are more masks and colored glass bottles and sea-related objects, a hobbyhorse, two exotic India music boxes of improbable structure and existence, and more at every turn of the head. Several separated structures connected by interesting steps of stone or wood, laced with vegetation in between, laid out along the hillside above the dead-end of the street. The street itself is very ordinary, even speaking of lower class and maybe poverty (not quite).

Bought postcard books that have scenes from the house. (Was not able to do this at Isla Negra because the gift shop was closed for "inventory," a bummer.)

Don't know about Neruda. Obviously very bright and artistic. Will read his poetry with enhanced awareness and study, knowing his "setting" better. But I think: he was so self-promoting, egotistical—yet he was creative, open-throttled, child-like in the freshness of embracing all. Neruda received only praise by the tour guides—nothing in the way of assessment or hint of criticism—all as it should be, of course. But what do you take away with you about Neruda? A lot, that's for sure, but it's like considering a long list of numbers—what does it add up to?

The pre-Columbian art museum was open but our time was much too short (about 1 hour). A really rich and well-presented collection. By far the best I remember seeing. (Can't remember specifics of the one in Mexico City some 40 years ago except that it was a major experience.) This one must be one of the world's premier pre-Columbian exhibits, displaying abundant information about the ancient South American and Central American cultures over thousands of years. It's hard to write impressions in a brief way when such powerful and fulsome representations spoke such volumes about the life on earth lived by many distinct and expressive cultures. They lived, they prospered, they died—and they left "this" legacy—with no intention of leaving a legacy, having had no intention of vanishing from the earth.

Went to the top of Santa Lucia "mountain"— a large park, ascended via a picturesque cobblestone road circling around the mountain, with many benches along the way, many of which were actively occupied by young lovers. It seemed to be a destination point for that purpose, and it was a pleasant touch. Parked at an upper level, then a considerable climb up various stages of stone steps. Made aware of a few signs that Charles Darwin was on this mountain during his famous Beagle voyage in the early 1800s.

At the top there was a complete panoramic view of Santiago—the first (the only one we had) such view of the whole far-reaching city of 6.5 million people. I made the first use of my new Sony movie camera (camcorder), panning 360 degrees. (I forgot that I could talk into the camera while shooting, so, after the panorama, I turned it on again to say what I had just filmed, taking an interesting view of my shoes while, again, forgetting that I was filming while I was talking. Oh well, it was my first go with any movie camera.) The height and views were exhilarating—a fitting way to begin to draw to a close the Chile and Santiago experience.

German left us at a restaurant in a neighborhood at the base of the funicular mountain featuring a number of restaurants. Floyd and I had a really superior dining experience at El Outre Sitio, one of two recommended by German. Started with a pisco sour (or was it two?), glass of wine, the best sea bass ever, lamb (we ordered differently and shared), a menu with wonderful choices (which we took as a remembrance, along with the table "Indian" adornment [with management's permission]).

A little shopping along the street, then a taxi to the hotel. Then packing etc. before the 7 p.m. reception for the first assembling of the Yale/Harvard Antarctica group. Then dinner with a "happy new year" under-theme. Talk to the group about tomorrow's departure—6 a.m., bags outside the room tonight by 1 a.m., etc. Saw one couple from San Antonio, Curtis and Phylis Vaughan, whom I know from the McDonald Observatory Board of Visitors that he and I share. He's a Harvard grad. I wear a Harvard badge (as a Harvard Law School grad), even though I went to Yale undergraduate. (When I called Yale to sign up, I could be placed on a waiting list, so I called Harvard and got on. This was the story I had to tell [to "explain"] several times on the tour when someone learned I was a Yalie and wanted to know why I was wearing a Harvard tag. Yalie ingenuity all the Yalies said.) Went to sleep about 11, but awakened at about midnight by the sound of what at first sounded like canons and war on the streets of Santiago, only to quickly realize that it was midnight on December 31. There was obviously some big-time fireworks display going on but not visible from our room, from which I could hear the fireworks and see the evidence of flashing lights of fireworks, but not the thing itself. I walked down the hall to have a view of another direction but still the same, and decided that I would have to get dressed etc. to find a place to have a view. Too sleepy, and the knowledge that there was a 4:30 wake-up call a-coming.

Thursday, January 1, 2004

Yes, it's the first day of 2004, awaking in room 1305 of the Hyatt Regency Hotel in Santiago, Chile. After the reception and dinner last night, did the packing and decided what to hold out to wear, what would be in our carry-on bags etc. for the early morning departure.

So, breakfast at 5, bus boarding at 6, arrival at the airport at 7, departure at 8:30 for a 3.5 hour flight to Ushuaia, to board the ship at about 4 or so. (I write this portion on the plane. On the bus, sat next to the wife of the ship captain. She has just arrived from Germany as a New Year's "present" (she said) for her husband. She speculated that our early departure—which had puzzled me—may be due to the scarcity of landing "slots" when the plane returns in the afternoon from Ushuaia, bearing the load of passengers who will disembark today from the same ship Orion which returned during the night from a 10-day trip to the Antarctica Peninsular—
the same trip that our group will begin this afternoon.)

Generally in this journal I will not try to embellish on my report on the people I am meeting and related conversations, and will note only a few. Floyd (Duke, '52) is sitting to my right. Elmer Johnson to my left. Yale class of '54. (My class was '53.) From Chicago, a lawyer with various pages in his life. We have talked mostly of his 3½ years as head of the Aspen Institute, and I have learned more about its mission(s), structure and activities. Earlier visited with another Yalie ('51), Bill Henry, also a lawyer, from Memphis, who spent years in Washington (including fox-hunting in Virginia for 8 years), knew a lot about the Memphis life insurance company with which I engaged in a major (for my company) acquisition transaction in 1998. Anyway, this kind of interaction will continue and will be interesting along the way, as I peer out at penguins, seals, whales, icebergs, the Southern Ocean, the Antarctic Peninsular and related archipelago.

The view from the window of the plane: we are apparently following the Andes chain to the colder south. More and more snow held in the upper reaches of the mountains, gleaming from what appears as a dark—almost black—fill-in of the lower portions of the meandering canyons and valleys.

After landing, 3 buses of us to a ski lodge about 30 minutes away. Lunch specialty of roasted lamb (sheep being a prevalent agronomy product), salad and coffee. A stop for a view of snow-covered mountains and to make photos. (Just one of many possible spots for viewing this spectacular piece of our earth.)

Then to Orion. A new white multi-deck passenger ship recently built in Germany, capacity of 107 passengers, 60 or so crew and staff. Very commodious rooms and all. A lovely feeling of comfort and snugness. An efficient and smooth boarding, etc. Talks, life jacket drill, tea, cocktails, dinner. For some reason, a late weighing of the anchor.

Set sail at 9:30! Marvelous! Dusk-quality hovering light. Cloudy. Misting a cold thin rain. Mountains along either side, monitoring the beginning of our journey beginning through the Beagle Channel toward Antarctica, 633 miles to our first destination: Elephant Island, across the Drake Passage. Stood on the 6th deck bow of the ship. The steady blow of steady wet rain touching down upon my face as the ship moves into a gentle but firming wind. The poem: *Oh westward wind, when wilt thou blow, that the fine rain down can rain. Christ, that I were in my lover's arms, and in my bed again.* So I was feeling the raining down of fine rain. (Not too fine, actually, even though I was remembering these lines. The rain had almost a sleet feeling—not exactly, just the hint. Enough to stimulate the skin's pleasure.) Someone along side me remarking about Cook and Drake and Darwin, and sailors on ships in those days, their little ships, plying through windy and freezing seas, how exposed, discomforted, brave, remarkable. And I thought, yes, and why? And I knew why.

This was not a common anytime moment. This was sailing out of Ushuaia, out of the Beagle

Channel, into the water not far south of the Magellan Strait, into the direction of Drake Passage, at fading light at 23 degrees S latitude, 71 degrees N longitude, under the overhang of immeasurably thick mist-cloud-sky, light dollops of rain spraying my face, cold weather, drizzle, ship moving, going south out of Tierra del Fuego.

This is the end of January 1, and the end of the beginning of the trip to Antarctica.

Friday, January 2

My mama dun rocked me in the cradle. Asleep at midnight to 8:30 without any sense of what or where, it was that sound! Within a minute of waking, feeling the gentle rhythmic undulating sway, realizing I was at sea, glancing out of the moisture-ladened porthole at the rippling gray expanse of water dimly rimmed by the misty gray overhang of an infinity-like sky, I had these lines in my head from a Harry Bellefonte version of the *Cotton Fields Back Home* ballad that I heard in the 50s. I realized that my ship-bed had been cradle-like, rocked by the Drake, and also thought: *out of the cradle, endlessly rocking* (Walt Whitman). Having slept only 4½ hours the night before, traveling and arriving the day before, late retiring, tired and happy. Who would not sleep profoundly? And wake with fullness?

Floyd was up and said that the breakfast period would end at 9. So I quickly dressed. The dining room was lively with happy breakfast chattering. Plentiful buffet. Seated near a large porthole window (the dining room was on the same level C as our room), near the more stable stern section of the ship). A swaying picture of sameness sea, with the floor (deck) and anchored chair buoyed upon a silent, slow, heaving and sinking. I fed a famished viscerality that we know well as a satisfying appeasement of hunger.

Moved right along, however, to a 9 a.m. meeting on the 4th level deck at the ship's stern to join a group with a naturalist for animal watching. When I arrived there were some 12 people, 2 naturalists with bird books for pictures and references. Soon saw a pintado (spelling ?) petrel sailing over the long white-water, churney wake of our ship, catching up to us. Then another, completing the pair. They played across the canvas sky just off our stern, ceaselessly swooping and turning: up, around, down, across, away, return, up, over, down. Never (almost never) a wing-flap. Perpetual wing-sailing. Then briefly a come-and-gone black browed albatross (about 4 feet wing span). The pintado petrels have white blotches across a blackness on the topside of the wing span (about one meter), thus their name, with a white underside. (I will not try to give much detail of wildlife sightings, generally, better left to the practice of the naturalists, but occasionally just a few words to capture identities. Also my measurement estimates are suspect.)

(I was writing this in the Library when the speaker system announced the beginning of 2 presentations on the 6th deck Cosmos Lecture Room. Meg Urry, a Yale astrophysicist/ astronomer, to talk about black holes, etc. Paul Horowitz, Harvard, etc. Can't take the time now to dwell on this. Returned afterwards to the Library [noon] to write again.)

This will have to be random. So much is happening. No time to write.

So, the above 2 lectures (good Q & A) ended at noon. To the Library to view, feel and write, 'til 12:30. Lunch 'til 1:30 because of interesting visits. Mike, an anthropology professor at Yale for over 40 years, recently switching his focus from Central and South America to Cambodia, etc. (Visited with him also yesterday.) Another chat with a lawyer with the Brown, Wood N. Y. law firm (which now has a new name due to a merger), same firm as Charlie Johnson, my Yale roommate; they knew each other. The firm had fabulous offices (which I visited) in the World Trade Center (lost only 1 employee on 9-11). We talked about careers, law, commuting, etc.

1:30 gathering in Cosmos for a naturalist lecture on Antarctica—what to expect. All lectures enriched with the marvels of PowerPoint. Q & A about winds, currents, Andes extension to the south re-appearing in (as?) Falklands, South Georgia, South Shetlands, archipelago near the Peninsular, and mountains of Antarctica itself. Slides of seals, penguins of the season (breeding), where we are located on the map "now," temperatures, wind chill factor.

Walking about the ship you don't have to be drunk to walk like a drunken sailor. The crossing so far is quite smooth (compared to what? Usual Drake crossings?) There is a constant rocking, slow, easy, rhythmic, interspersed with bits of suddennesses (that get your attention).

Need to get more acquainted with my cameras. I had intended to have this "crossing" time to read the manuals and inspect the buttons and settings, but no time yet. One lecture this morning by Horowitz was on photographing landscapes—Adam Ansel problems, trade-offs of light and shadow, detail at zoom, F stops and exposures, what do you want the picture to say (and be willing to compromise the rest). The problem: Why is my photograph not like what I saw?

All along I am trying to find time to work on poems—one in particular. About constant change. So what is existence if change is continuous? Nothing ever remains the same. And puzzling over a line: *Then what is this but a useless ball?* I wonder, why did I insert that line? I did, and it belongs, almost like a keystone. But what does it have to do with the poem? What is a poem and how does it work? I like the content, the penetrating, the satisfying surge, especially the quick emotional slide-back from the surge when the last line is said. Beforehand I thought that the trip might provide poetry-writing moments, and I brought a small sheaf of poems-in-progress, including the "change" poem. But the opposite is true. During the trip I can't even work on the poems that I have begun, with so much "coming in." And "change"? What is Antarctica? Change? And changelessness? Millions of years of accumulations of fresh-water ice. A buried continent, holding information about the earth's ancient past. Change but no change. Millions of years ago, one big continent (including what is now Antarctica, Africa, South America, India, Australia, and New Zealand, known as Gondwana, which began its break-up some 180 million years ago). Former times of temperate climates. But step back to the long zoom. Nothing stays the same. And we are microscopically dotted here. Here?

The ship's engines hum. A never-ending hum, a continuous under-water, muffled roar. Oscillating hum with pitches interacting with the force of what the ship's bow is doing with the plowing over the ragged sea-top. A long continuing string of extruded heaving, feeling like something that is not ever meant to stop. The ocean holds us, a ship we are, washing on its mighty surface, up and down, heave and ho, slow and o' o' o', sudden rescues when that which held us dropped away, then it returns, pushing us up, to shift us over, then go away again, then re-appear, full and strong. A little ship, filled with 170 people, a tiny dot at approximately 57 degrees 13 minutes south by 63 degrees, 10 minutes west on this gigantic globe, where the ocean is the palm of an uncertain hand.

A lecture by Meg Urry on black holes, her special subject. Very well done with a good Q & A. But the question was discussed on ship here and there: why does an Antarctica trip feature astronomers? These are great subjects and very qualified presenters. But the specialties should be subjects like geology, plate tectonics, icebergs, glaciers, wild life in Antarctica (of which we have talks, but from people not nearly as credentialed as the 2 astronomers, our top-billed lecturers, and not enough), evolution of animal life in Antarctica, and other subjects. The more this comes up, the stranger it seems.

Had dinner with Curtis and Phyllis Vaughan (the couple from San Antonio), and a couple from Boston (Jordan and Sandy Golding). Curtis and Jordan were classmates at Harvard College and then the Business School, but met for the first time on this trip. Good conversations about black holes, astronomy, limits of knowledge (pre-black holes, other universes, etc.) Yes, this was interesting but we might have been (should have been) talking about Antarctica subjects.

Jordan and I made a visit to the ship's bridge. Impressive array of instrumentation, wide-wide windshield view of the bow plowing across a dark sea, plunging through wave after wave of churning, flapping water. 5 CPR screens, operator chairs, panels, knobs and switches, 3 men who knew virtually no

English so they let us marvel and tried to answer questions (so not much conversation).

In the cabin. Some progress in reading the camcorder manual before the beginning of sleep.

Saturday, January 3

Second day push-humming along the sea-surface, cutting and gliding, opening up and parting foaming slices of waves, 14 plus knots at this steady speed, onward, onward. The second day is much like the first. Dining room, lecture hall, Leda lounge for briefing about the IAATA (International Association of Antarctica Tours Association) for a membership-mandated recitation of ecology rules, and information about the Antarctica Treaty formed in 1959, signed by numerous nations. The IAATA has numerous tour-operator members (sorry, don't recall the number) which is a self-regulating association pledged to protecting the environment of Antarctica while allowing visitations by tourists. Instructions and information about the zodiacs, boardings and landings procedures, etc.

Then a trip "below" to the "mud room" to perform a decontamination of boots, assignment of cubicles where the boots remain while on board, put on just before boarding, and taken off and cleaned upon return to the ship from a zodiac "landing." Decontaminating is a disinfecting dipping of boots, new and old, to ward off possibilities of contaminants.

Lunch. Then an old, reconstituted film (*South*) actually shot on Shackleton's voyage, ending in the rescue from Elephant Island. This is the island to which our ship Orion is bound as I write.

Now, after 20 minutes "respite" we go back to the lecture room for Meg Urry's talk on the "Highlights from the Hubble Space Telescope." Before joining the Yale faculty 3½ years ago, Meg spent 14 years working with Hubble at the Space Telescope Science Institute in Baltimore. Meg's lecture focused (no pun) on presentation of beautiful Hubble photographs, reciting the mirror problem, its fix, logistics, future, planned "next" space telescope (2017) if it happens. A usual good Q & A. Break for standard tea time (5 – 5:45).

The first iceberg. While at tea, looking at my camcorder manual, I filmed the Leda Lounge tea, finding out about the "nightshot" (low light) button. Then the bridge announced that on the port side the first iceberg could be seen. I went to the outside stern deck and started my camera on the iceberg—discovered also that the weather was much colder than when I last sampled it (we're headed toward "colder"), and there was some rain. I quickly stepped into a protected area (but still outside) and filmed through the water-laced windowpane, hopefully capturing the first iceberg sighting. Also thinking: yes, the weather may be cold when we visit Elephant Island tomorrow morning.

At 6 p.m. there was a talk with slides to anticipate our expected arrival at Elephant Island. A 45-minute zodiac cruise close to the spot where the Shackleton group landed. Then the ship will move around the island to Cape Lookout for a zodiac trip ashore (landing). Information about group arrangements, etc., and what to wear. Possibilities that changes might occur depending on weather and ice.

Dinner at the invitation of Bob Doyle who arranged a table, including his daughter Alicia (recently out of college, doing research work at a Boston hospital), Professor Paul Horowitz (the Harvard lecturer) and his wife (a physician from Iran) and Mr. And Mrs. Sykes (retired business man from Buffalo, N.Y.) Bob is on the faculty (administrative staff?) doing alumni PR work on this trip. An interesting group and discussion. Horowitz struck me as a Woody Allen type. Has Woody Allen mannerisms and he can be very funny in his lectures, and in the visit. Quite bright and knowledgeable.

Arranging things in the cabin, packing, etc. for the first "landing" tomorrow morning, then bed.

Sunday, January 4

Breakfast, to the room, hear the announcement that we are arriving at Elephant Island. Grab camera, go to deck 6 and exit to starboard side near the bow. The scene has everything that I came for. Sharp, uprising black and white land with a small island look, yet there is a huge, monstrous, white, gleaming glacier way up in the distant high place. Substantial icebergs in several places about the panorama of the ship. Took movies. Soon thereafter, dressed in too much clothing because what it will be like is uncertain, board a zodiac. (The Yale people were boarding first and since I had shown up early, I boarded with the Yale group, so Floyd will be a on a later zodiac. I won't go into the organization procedure, which will change, and it doesn't matter. It worked well.)

Mostly cloudy but patches of blue sky. Zodiac bouncing and swaying and riding the undulating waves. Under way, soon coming near the Shackleton monument spot (Point Wild), thinking about the story of their journey to find "rescue" on this small, desolate, isolated piece of earth. (Point Wild, named for Frank Wild, the leader of the 22 men who remained stranded on this spot while Shackleton and two others sailed in one of the small boats 800 miles to South Georgia, to return months later to the men, awaiting rescue.)

Penguins gathered in several clusters on ledges, etc. Birds active, mostly petrels but several albatrosses, feeding and swooping. Looking back at Orion, a beautiful ship, with a large iceberg (as high as, and longer than, the ship) just to the stern and behind Orion. Kind of intoxicating.

Next a lecture on penguins. Good PowerPoint pictures. A spunky young Spanish-speaking woman (naturalist) struggling with her English (but successfully so). She opened by singing a stanza from *Don't Cry For Me Argentina*, a really nice voice that won a big applause. So we saw and heard much about the 17 species of penguins, obviously zeroing in on the Antarctic ones—like the Emperor, Adelie, Chintoos, Chinstraps, Macaronis. If you ever sit down to read about penguins (with pictures) chances are you would thumb right on through the pages. Here, however, I just saw hundreds of penguins in groups on ledges and shores of Elephant Island, and penguins porpoising through the water, and the foreknowledge that there is much more to come, starting with a landing (the first) scheduled for 2:30 this afternoon (the "other side" of Elephant Island, to which we are not steaming). Therefore the lecture had immediate meaningfulness and interest, and penguins are truly remarkable, interesting and wonderful birds.

Lunch after the lecture. Sat with Ross Siragusa. There are 9 in his family group on the trip. Discovered that his father was Yale '53 (my class) and met him (and wife) at the end of the lunch. Father was treating 3 generations to the Antarctica expedition—a way to bring the family together for Christmas and New Year.

First the naturalists took zodiacs ashore to assess—exactly what I never heard. About 1 hour behind schedule we began the zodiac boarding procedures for Cape Lookout. I have photographs to attest to the spectacular geographic protrusions and water expanse and passageways. I can now attest to the pleasure of the zodiac transfer from ship to shore, the bouncing of the zodiac, the bird strokes painted in live action across the snow-streaked "mountain" sides and watery slopes of sea-waves. Boots in water as I stepped off the zodiac onto the terra firma. (After 3 days of the ship's endless motion, the fact that the ground did not move was a moment to register.) There were plenty of penguins grouped and strolling and gawking at us. An elephant seal stretched out languidly on the top of a rise and rocky area. Up the side of the mountain, more penguins looking down at us and undoubtedly having quite a chat. Occasionally one group or another burst into penguin-chorusing—a squeally, clatterly, squawkerly clustering of noisiness. They raised their beaks at the end of their up-stretched necks to bleat it all to the sky. Made snapshots and motion pictures, as did Floyd. Petrels, albatrosses, penguins, seals and frequent unidentified birds making themselves at home in this home of theirs while a small crowd of red-parka human types puttered around a small rocky shore of one of nature's naked places.

The zodiac ride back to the ship (about a 15 minute trip) had to plow across some feisty swells, thrashing up sudden bursts of spray, smacking down from a swell that drops the boat in fleeting free-fall, making a labor out of the way back to the ship.

Now as I write I have finished a cup of tea, sitting in the Leda lounge by a big window out of which is a scene that is as old as the earth but striking me as fresh newness. The ship's engines have cranked up and we are now making way, headed 158 miles to Hope Bay at the north tip of the Peninsular, sometime tomorrow.

I will share here an "image" that entered my mind: a ship arriving at Elephant Island, filled with penguins as passengers, crowding along the rails of the decks, all dressed up in black and white, eagerly looking and pointing, as they arrive to view the clusters of humans on the island, standing in small groups and strolling here and there, to the delight of the passenger penguins.

The announcements at the 7 p.m. cocktails before the Captain's dinner forecast tomorrow's schedule of arriving at Hope Bay to touch foot on the Antarctic Continent. Due to ice, some ships may not be getting through, so, it was said, we will have to wait and see.

The Captain's dinner at 7:45. A good menu with choices—wine is served every day for lunch and dinner—and caviar, mushroom soup, lobster tail, chocolate mouse and coffee. Not bad for a stretch of Southern Ocean between Elephant Island and the Antarctica Peninsular. An interesting table. A black lawyer from San Diego (Yale Law School), 2 women traveling solo (one married) and the young tour manager, Alex (Harvard '02). He's worked for Travel Dynamics since last spring and sought this tour because it gave him the opportunity to visit (re-visit) Chile where he lived from age 5 to 13. He talked of his pleasure of hearing and resuming the Chilean Spanish (his parents are Cuban; he lives in New Jersey) which he says (he now realizes) has more music in its content than any other Spanish with which he is acquainted. This led to the topic of the 2 Chilean poets who have received the Nobel Prize, and possibly this quality of Chilean Spanish has something to do with it.

And while we talked, through the window was the sea garnished with icebergs.

11 p.m. dressed for bed. And writing this. Returned from the Leda Lounge where a trio played music and several (with increasing numbers) gathered after the Captain's dinner. Note the time. It is not yet dark. Sitting and listening to music from Russia, Ukraine, Odessa and Gypsy—this trio from Russia (they spoke Russian, and 2 or 3 women from the audience spoke to them in Russian requesting specific songs). (I confess to trying my "hand" at dancing to the dance-provoking Russian folk-dance music with Mrs. Horowitz who was up and at'um.) And looking out the window at passing icebergs and scraps of ice, almost an eerie, surreal light, certainly for sure a scene that to me was arresting and astounding, sitting and listening and looking, feeling the rocking embrace of a warm ship.

I was thinking, maybe there is some way to re-set the day's clock to 9 a.m. and do it again.

Monday, January 5, 2004

This is an eyewitness account. This morning, awakened about 5:30 by bursts of short growls of the engines, revving up, maneuvering. Looked out the window into a dense field of ice, noting one hugh iceberg nearby. So I quickly dressed, grabbed my movie camera and headed for the bow of the 6th deck. In this brief 20 minutes the ship had completed "backing off" from the ice field encountered while attempting to get into Hope Bay but now had turned its bow toward King George Island.

(This information I received about 1 hour later. When first viewing and shooting the ice and the distant land mass I thought it was the Peninsular tip of Antarctica. The Captain had said last evening that ships were not getting through the channel but the Orion would give it a try. Apparently not successful.)

The thoughts I had when I first looked out my room's porthole at 5:30 involved Shackleton's fate (although I did not think we were "trapped"—only the occasion for the thought). I thought: are we being "Shackletoned"? Then realized for the first time the irony of his name—that his ship Endurance was "shackled" by the ice—and it shackled a "ton."

A presentation in Cosmos by Adam, a young Swedish naturalist (accent and all) on the Swedish Antarctica expedition (1903) on which everything went wrong until some 9 months later, through a miraculous stroke of timing, they were rescued. Adam lost his PowerPoint and had to improvise, which he did with wonderful talent, to everyone's delight.

Zodiac excursion—10 to noon—to Penguin Island. Returned and now sitting in the Library 4th deck looking at the iceberg-studded seascape. Plenty of penguins on Penguin Island (mostly Chinstraps) and a number of seals (Elephant seal and one big male fur seal). A rookery for giant petrels was nearby so lots of petrels going to and fro the nests. Giant petrels are as large as the small version of the albatrosses (and at first I thought I was watching albatrosses playing in the air).

Took movies and still shots on the landing. Someone got me and Floyd together with my camera. As Floyd and I were approaching the point for re-mounting the zodiac through a field of plentiful fresh snow, I could not resist, so I made a snowball and got him on my first shot. He returned the favor, and we had a brief shoot-out.

The zodiac return. The water is slate blue and the icebergs are white white. Actually some icebergs do have streaks and patches of marble blue. As we know, compressed ice turns blue over time. A ghosty shining blue that sort of quietly screams out from the depth of the iceberg, gem-like. Saw some penguins porpoising, zipping through the water. (Do porpoises ever "penquin"?) The whomp and frolic of the zodiac, spray splashing on us. Then the iffy ascent by quick hopeful steps from the zodiac's floor to the mounting block to the zodiac's outer inflated rim to the ship's loading dock, with the zodiac operator helping to send you, and 2 dock guys helping to receive you, clasping hand-on-wrist fashion (the instructed grip) and trying to catch the zodiac on its wave-ride up, but not the sinking one (or else the step to the dock is a lulu).

In the mud room there are seats and short hoses for rinsing off the mud and penguin guano, and then the boots are stowed in cubicles (in exchange for sneakers). Floyd and I returned to the room (317) and in the process of taking off coats, cameras, etc., I realized I had become disconnected from my binoculars. (My trips ashore, so far, involved 2 cameras and a pair of binoculars strapped around my neck.) I went back to the zodiac loading dock and passed the word of my loss, so hopefully someone spotted them (it?) and they will be returned. Otherwise it will be obligatory that I return to this place. (If we see, as we sail away, a penguin looking at us through binoculars we'll know who the thief was, I will note carefully what he looks like, and I will catch the thief upon my return.)

Read the "Times Digest" which appears each day in the Library. The U.S. Mars probe (*Spirit*) made a perfect landing. Pretty exciting. News (for me) of its first communications (televised) will have to wait one week.

This afternoon, went ashore on King George Island, a Polish Research site. Penguins by the hundreds, maybe thousands. Chinstraps and Adelies. Very rocky, very picturesque setting. All around, icebergs, mountains, snow slopes and extensive white vistas of white regions beyond. While walking along the rocky shoreline penguins suddenly began popping out of the water, deftly "plopping" feet-first right on the shore after the "pop" out of the water. Some 15 penguins, popping and plopping, one after another. Then they waddle-walked along the beach, headed toward the rookery up to a next plateau, which was up the hill a ways, onto a higher elevation, a slope of penguins, dotted like a Surrat painting of penguin land. They walk upright—Penguin Erectus. Don't know if they achieved this before homo. They are entirely confident of their mastery of the upright walking.

And I, walking along the beach alone, slowly, upright—marveling at the footing totally covered in small (3, 6, 10 inches in diameter) stones, smooth from untold years of nature's rubbing—spliced, speckled, clean, multi-layered specimen of eras and eras of geological dynamics. How I longed to be able to read the stories of earth's history held tight in the bodies of these eclectic stones, and yet the stories were there: beautiful, crooked, smooth, layered, tortured—written literally in stone. These penguins, these whales, these birds, these seals, these stones, these mountains, these seas—a soft rain was sprinkling, and light moved in and out of the clouds frothing above out heads, listening to the lapping of the seashore.

My binoculars had been found and returned, so I feel badly that I had the thought of penguin thievery.

Dinner with Dr. Jordan and Carole Cohen, and two traveling-alone women, Vienna and Martha. Jordan was in Elihu, class of '57. (I was a member of the '53 delegation.) Vienna was at the Yale Drama School, '57 era. After years of success in acting, she changed to become an Episcopalian priest, a sort of female pioneer in this field, and taught at the seminary in Virginia. And on and on, too much to record, as we exchanged ideas, personals, etc.

So here I am, 9:30 p.m., still daylight. Floyd has joined "the others" in the Cosmos Lecture Room for the movie *Endurance*, and I decided to pass (having seen it) even though it's very relevant to where we are. But I was up at 5:30 and it's been a long day. The lecture room is always too warm and I'd fall asleep, probably. Tomorrow we will zodiac to Half Moon Island (part of South Shetland Group) starting at 8:30, unusually early. Steaming there tonight as we sleep.

Tuesday, January 6, 2004

Up at 6:30, coffee and a little movie-making on the stern and bow, viewing Half Moon Island, where we are now anchored. Also known as Livingston Island, which is the largest of the South Shetland Islands, south of King George Island. About 62 something south latitude and 57 or so west longitude (if I remember today's announcement correctly).

An early disembarkation after breakfast to Half Moon Island, the plan being to have everyone back on board by 11 a.m. in order to sail on to Aitcho Island—for the afternoon landing. Half Moon Island has lots of snow, so the climb from the zodiac landing up the slope to a top mid-ridge involved frequent sudden foot-sinks, occasionally destabilizing a person. There are two major knobs rising out of the snow at the "top" which was dense with Chinstrap penguins nesting on stone-bed nests. Little chicks were in there somewhere. Saw one penguin chasing another fairly aggressively (caught him/her briefly), apparently because the fleeing one had stolen a stone from the nest of the chasing one. The noise was rich, heads of speaking penguins beaked upward in an appeal to the sky, a barking/baying/honking sound. When they all join the chorus, it is noisy. Couldn't say whether they were complaining about our presence or displaying territorial defense (which is, sort of, the same).

In the bay separating our land and a much larger mass, the water was very very still and almost mirror-like. Someone said it was especially krill-rich, so, with my binoculars, I scanned for whales. Saw lots of porpoising penguins, some seals moving around and long lines of water streaks indicating that something was moving beneath the surface. But no whales unless I decide to lie.

I write this at 10:45 a.m. sitting in the Library, having read the Times Digest. Afghanistan, Martha Stewart trial, letter bombs from Italy, U.S. presidential race news, Medicare, discovery of brightest star ever, etc. What is all that?

11:30 to 12:30 lecture by Meg Urry's husband on use of super-cooled apparatus placed in a satellite to detect and measure X-rays. I thought during the lecture how I would have preferred some information about the island and animals that we just saw.

Lunch with Dr. Scott Johnson and son, Craig, from San Antonio, and a doctor and wife from N.Y.—both Yalies. Met at 2 to zodiac to Aitcho Island. Lots of good photographs. Dense with Gentoo penguins (as well as some Chinstraps), occasional seals lolling about. Went with a group of some 8 or so on a long trek (about 1 hour) up, around and over, past penguin nests, to the "far side" where the geology was spectacular. Upthrusts and high, sheer cliffs (and I was standing on one). Nesting of Giant Petrels and another large black bird about the size of the Giant Petrel, the name of which I did not catch.

Then a long, steep snow bank down which our Swedish naturalist slid, Shackleton fashion. I was second, with no hesitation, a fun snow-slide on my butt and back. Then several others. (I have some of it on film.) Nearby, at the base of a high monolithic upthrust standing all alone on a lovely shore, a small rookery of penguins, next to which some 10 or 12 large elephant seals sprawled out in a lumpy pile.

Then the trek back, walking snow paths, trying to find firm footing but always the occasional sudden sink of the foot. The boots work very well— a good, comfortable fit, ideal for the conditions which include snow, mud, pebbles, water.

On the zodiac return to the ship the fog had settled in. Impossible to see far. The penguins seemed especially active in their porpoising frolics, a gaggle doing it over here, then a bunch over there. I began to think, does the zodiac operator know her way for sure? Everybody very quiet. We motored on and on, nothing in sight beyond the immediate water and pieces of ice. Then a ghost ship, shrouded in thick fog. Beginning at about this fog-stage, the zodiacs began to travel in pairs or more, not to get lost.

A shower, fresh change, Floyd and I had tea in the Library, as the ship gets under way. 5:45. Two thoroughly enjoyable excursions.

At 7 p.m., gathered with everybody in the Leda Lounge (end of cocktail hour) for briefing and debriefing. Tomorrow will be a busy day. Just before this began, a whale (humpback) was sighted on port side and everyone rushed to it, including me. But I did not see the whale. Some did, some didn't.

Dinner: Floyd, myself, Elmer and Connie Johnson. Pleasant. (Elmer is the one who was head of the Aspen Institute, my seatmate on the flight to Ushuaia.) Floyd to the movie, I to our room.

Wednesday, January 7, 2004

Entering the bay of Port Lockroy I filmed the embracing two arms of snow-covered watchful mountains lining both sides of our approach. Saw 3 or 4 whales—not sure of the type: small, 2 together, then nearby there was one (maybe 2), briefly breaking the surface in an otherwise mirror-still black film of ice-strewn water.

The sun sporadically breaking through with not-so-bright light, but a welcome sight—seeming to fulfill the promise of an Antarctic summer. The giant snowfields along the row of mountains gleamed out optical shouts of whiteness.

A short-distance zodiac ride to Lockroy station, featuring a small building, a major portion of which is a room for souvenirs, postcards, maps, etc.—a simple modest display. Two British guys were the clerks, taking in dollars (which, along with British Sterling, are the only acceptable currencies). This historic research station was restored and now maintained by the British Antarctica Heritage Trust. Stays open about 4 months a year. I picked up a small brochure to read later what they do besides sell postcards. I mailed 8 (5 of which I purchased and wrote before, and bought 5 more at the station). Dropped the 8 in a letterbox, with Lockroy postage stamps (the only valid ones, per the mailbox message). Maybe they will even get delivered.

A zodiac excursion to a nearby spot, not a large area. Usual array of penguins but known for nesting of a cormorant colony. Surrounded by majestic mountains, displaying black lofts of volcanic upthrusts and fields of white. Saw (and heard) some calving from the long, large line of snow-cliffs across the bay. So far I had not witnessed any calving even though I had seen many long stretches of calved-off snow-cliffs, day after day. I had begun to think that this was simply not the "calving season" (who would resist?). But, as stated, I got my moment. Very thunderous sound, reverberating across the hugged-in bay.

Now, in the Library, having changed and downed 2 cups of hot, Tabasco-seasoned bouillon, I look out the window at the huge water-scape dominating the scene of water-ridged and cloud-banded sky that is called, let's say, a view from the Library porthole.

A lecture regarding Kennedy's assassination—specifically, the audio channel that a policeman had left open inadvertently, and how the final analysis of this eliminated the earlier implications of a thought-to-have-been shot from the grassy knoll. Reason? Professor Horowitz had served on a panel to make the revised study.

The Orion reached Lemaire Channel, the southernmost point of our journey, a rich, dramatic, scenic stretch of water, mountains on both sides, icebergs and ice all about. Much photographing. The Channel is 65 degrees and (estimated) 30 minutes south latitude, and the Antarctic Circles is 66 degrees and (estimated) 30 minutes south latitude. Too much ice up ahead, so we now turn to go north toward Paradise Bay, the continent itself.

The late afternoon landing at Paradise Bay. Very calm water, partly cloudy sky (which means heavy low clouds of massiveness). The station named Almirante Brown, an Argentine research station, has a few buildings neighbored by penguins. Beyond, there is a snowfield leading up a steep incline to a top perch—quite a steep climb. 15-20 people struggled and climbed to the tope, and several began to toboggan down Shackleton-fashion. I was one (captured on film). Floyd decided not to make the climb.

Here's a point. Landing at Paradise Bay was the first (and only) moment to set foot upon the continent of Antarctica. All of the rest of our landing sites are islands, which stretch in clusters along the western side of the Peninsular. Some discussion about whether, if you missed this landing, did you go to Antarctica? (If you are in Manhattan, are you in North America?) Certainly you will be in Antarctica, but, query, did you reach the continent of Antarctica?

Well, I did: Antarctica and the continent of Antarctica.

Antarctica, by the way, is not easy to define. One accepted definition is: all of that area south of 60 degrees south latitude.

Thursday, January 8, 2004

Today (morning): Deception Island. It's a circle of land around a bay, formed by volcanic eruptions. The circle has an opening, named Neptune's Bellows, through which ships may sail—carefully. Don't know the statistics, so I'll guess: a mile or two across the bay, longwise, and a little less the other way. High cliffty mountains (5-10,000 feet?, or higher in places) around the land mass, very volcanic in looks, with subtle color variations giving relief to the black landscape, some places of snow and ice. Neptune's Bellows has high cliff-sides. The shore-line is very beach-like, except the beach is black volcanic ash-sand.

The British established a whaling station here in the early part of the 1900s (20s). It fell into disuse in the early 30s (abandoned in 1931 I think). Along the beach area are vats and other whale oil processing equipment, some half buried, slowly vanishing.

An airplane hanger is up on one end of the area, with the fuselage of an Otter-type plane next to it. It was brought in for assembly but never completed. The whale oil enterprise declined precipitously about 1931, when a combination of depression and competition from new ships that were also on-board factories making whaling and oil processing more efficient (poor whales).

Some of the group took a hot-tub dip in the two holes dug in the sand for the occasion, quite near the water's edge. The water welling up in the holes is warm-to-hot. Based on preliminary information, they had put swimsuits on underneath, and a place behind a nearby structure was arranged for changing. A few of the younger ones also switched from dipping in the cold cold Antarctic water, back into the warm water. Fun and frolic.

One strange fact to note: no animals. An occasional bird (petrel?) but nothing else. A naturalist said penguins were on the outer side of the surrounding rim. When we were zodiacing back to the ship I saw 3 penguins on a distant inner shore, taking a stroll on the beach.

Now, back on board, in the Library, drinking bouillon, writing, looking out the window at the Deception Island landscape that has a surreal, "other-world," quality—the moon or who knows? Also it happens that there is a continuing quietness—no engines, no talking—only an occasional barely audible voice from below. The ship at anchor is slowly revolving drifting-wise around its anchor, moving the landscape in slow turning motion. Quite a moment to savor. Ice and fire, right here on Deception Island. (The last eruption was 1970. The next one scheduled for January 9 or 10, 2004, more or less.)

Captain Gartner made a slide presentation in the Leda Lounge on the building of the Orion. A fine ship, complete with stabilizers to help suppress the rolling in the crossing of the Drake.

After lunch, a talk on marine mammals. Very interesting. Seals, whales, etc.

Than a landing on Hannah Point at Livingston Island—the last landing of our trip. It treated us right. The zodiac transfer was wet and rough, a cold wind with light rain. On shore the weather eased, but still occasional light rain feeling sleet-like. A fairly strong wind with occasional brief respite. Penguins galore. Chinstraps mostly but also Adelies. Walked along the long beach in a group with a naturalist, encountering clusters of Elephant Seals who pile up in close quarters, say some 15-20 in a cluster. Several instances of seals in the water, frolicking or something. They are huge animals, with an extraordinarily wide mouth-opening that rolls and growls out a staccato lung-powered offering like a car engine trying to start.

The penguin nests featured small chicks, about 8-12 inches tall. The Chinstraps have 2 each—furry gray plump cute birds. The Adelies have one, for which there's an explanation. Albatrosses contending against the wind, sometimes stationery at a forward-stance standoff, at times actually receding as though gliding backward as the wind wins the face-off.

Someone at dinner said it's strange but true that if there's any animal that you have to have too many of, you would want it to be penguins.

What a fine way to end our shore excursions. The weather had been pretty friendly all week. Today was not overly harsh but it certainly gave us the opportunity to appreciate our parkas, hoods, gloves, wet covers and boots. (We walked through several rapid-flowing streams of 3-4 feet widths and 6-10 inches deep.) The penguins, seals, petrels, albatrosses, weather and over-arching scenery collaborated to wish us farewell.

The zodiac return to the ship was filled with spray, pitching and whamming the water. We had to make 3 approaches to the landing dock because the waves were so contentious. When finally latched onto the dock the zodiac had its lurching spasms to make the step-off a moment for concentration.

Floyd and I had our showers, then to the Leda Lounge for a drink. My first hard liquor on board: Tullamore Dew, the best ever. After about 30 minutes or so, a whale sighting on the starboard side was announced. Sure enough, two humpback whales had appeared for the sole purpose of putting on a whale of a show. They blew and they arched and they rose skyward out of the water to smack magnificently to the water again. Breaching in giant dimensions. When one would come up, bringing up with it a floral spray of white water, the voices in the room would rise with the whale—extended exclamations of 'ah's and 'aw's as the whale pounded itself back into its ocean bed, in sync with the dying of our unison voices. The flukes were waved, and they frolicked, as the ship placed them slowly to the stern, and the crowd moved outside to the stern's deck. When—would you believe it?—two more humpbacks appeared on the port side near the stern. Enough already! It ended and everybody was thrilled, saying things like: best whale sighting I've ever seen.

The rest of the evening. Yale and Harvard alumni associations had separate 1-hour cocktail parties for reports, etc. Floyd and I stayed in the Leda Lounge Harvard Group. Then dinner—Thai food because the chef has had a Thai culinary background experience and wanted to show off. It was okay.

Now, in my room, the ship has begun its Drake crossing behavior which I experienced on the first 2 days. Rolling, pitching, straining engines, large white parting water-waves thrown off by the ship revved up to about 15 knots. Announcement said we may have some rough seas. One passenger at our dinner table lefty suddenly, and her husband left a little later to check on her, speculating possible sea sickness. Barf bags placed handily along the hallway rails. As for me, lying now in bed, feeling the sinking and rising, the heaving and swaying, and enjoying it. Definitely some people experiencing seasickness, or, if you prefer, mal de mere.

Now it's going home. Thursday night, all day Friday and Saturday, arrival at Ushuaia Sunday morning. Something about a stop on Isla Diego Remirez 430 miles from here, but it's not at all clear what this means.

Friday, January 9, 2004

At sea all night, awaking in the sinking, rising, swaying, and heaving. Walking is a problem. At breakfast, quite a challenge to walk with cereal and milk bowl in hand to a table. During breakfast, decided to practice while walking in the rooms and halls to try to walk without the aid of touching rails or walls or other supports. Stairways were the most difficult, but by practice it was achievable—as all sailors well know.

Went to the bridge and watched the ship's bow dive and rise as it led the groaning ship up and down the wave-swells and ocean-wells. The dynamically churning of sweeps, lifts, liquid geometries, white-cap appearances and vanishings, and big swelling rising rolls of on-coming walls of heaving water with no heed for the well-being of the ship's bow, and the bow fearlessly plowing straight at and into the pounding rolls of water, splashing huge frothing water spray, all airy, wet and powerful, against the wide-stretched windshield of the bridge. How the endless mass of sea crows out its lasting lust for unstoppable, chaotic ceaselessness.

At 10 a.m., a preview of information regarding arrival at Ushuaia (the pass by Isla Diego Remiras was cancelled due to schedule concerns), bags, bus trip in Tierra del Fuego Park, flight to Santiago, end of tour.

At 2, Professor Coe presented a History of Chocolate, a book he has published to complete the project of his late wife who focused on the role of food in studying anthropology. (Presentations had switched to the Leda Lounge, because it is on the 4th deck and somewhat more stable than the 6th deck Cosmos Lecture Room.)

At 4 in the Leda Lounge, a lecture by Meg Urry on the accelerating universe, the mysteries of dark matter, etc.

While having tea at 5:30 with Professor Coe, got word of wandering albatrosses sighted from the aft deck near us, so we went immediately. And we saw them. They are often spotted but this was my first. (The "wandering" albatross is the giant size.) All the time we are treated to petrels of various kinds, as Orion groans and pushes her way across the Drake Passage towards the tip of South America, where we will "round the Horn."

Saturday, January 10, 2004

Second day crossing the Drake. A little calmer. Understand the wind howled up strong last night but I slept through it. There is a slow-motion pitching to and fro, with some continuous rolling mixed in. Went to the mud room, did a final clean of my boots (and Floyd's) and brought them back to the room for packing, Bought penguin souvenirs from the gift shop. Arranged a Visa charge of a well-deserved gratuity for the staff. Generally thinking that packing is today. Now having coffee at 10 a.m. in the Leda Lounge after a brief aft deck look at petrels and black browed albatrosses. The soothing sea scene through the windows, cloud-gray sky with a barely-distinct undulating line dividing sea from sky.

Yesterday Floyd and I took a tour of the engine room. Kind of massive, big mechanical set-ups and connections. Rows of switches and lights. Talk of statistics such as thrust and kilowatts. Pretty mundane. It's just the heart that makes us go.

I return to this just after having seen Cape Horn at approximately 3 p.m. Passengers have been on advice not to go on deck because the wind is about 40 knots, kicking up heavy spray and blasts of ocean-water. Thick clouds hanging low presenting a very foggy/cloudy Cape Horn. It could be made out, a bell shape mountain, in ghostly outline. The snapshot just couldn't bring it up, and others were having the same luck (lack of). My binoculars enhanced the view quite a bit. Sailing westerly, Cape Horn off our left side. It took me a long time, but I sailed around the Horn.

Before Cape Horn, Floyd and I were in the Cosmos Lecture Room for a film and talk on albatrosses and "long fishing lines." The latter is the fishing strategy involving miles and miles of a baited line which is then reeled in to harvest the catch. Estimated 20,000 albatrosses per year are killed by this process. The speaker said he thinks the number is twice as high. There are organizations trying to solve this.

Sunday, January 11, 2004

Yesterday continued through tea, the Captain's Farewell Cocktail gathering and dinner (coat and tie). Parting remarks and applause as various staff, medical doctor, captain, tour manager, etc., were presented for thanks. Very good menu of choices, wine as usual. Packing chore with intent to be packed by bedtime, anticipating a 5:30 wake-up call, bags outside cabin by 7, breakfast 6:30-8:00, disembarkation to buses at 8:30.

We were informed that, during the afternoon of the day before, wind rose to a steady 50 knots, gusts up to 65. The ship was taking a beating as we all had noticed. At times the 4th deck portholes were totally covered over by the smack of a huge wave-wall of water accompanied by spontaneous ooo's and oh's bouncing from the startled crowd. Waves were running as high as 20-30 feet, or more. Everybody confined to the interior. But, amazingly, appearances of birds continued their sailing presence outside the windows.

Awakened this morning at 5:15 by the ship engines revving up, dying off, as the ship was maneuvering into docking position. There were about 6 large ships, mostly Orion size, but one, *The World*, was a behemoth, and I wondered whether this huge thing visited Antarctica. Floyd thought it was a condominium ship that stays in motion around the globe.

The three buses took us on a tour of the Tierra del Fuego National Park. A wonderful excursion. Misty, thin, non-wetting drizzle, somewhat cold (I had on Houston weather clothes for the travel ahead, with a sweater, fortunately, and many others still wore their red Orion parkas, headed for destinations in the north of North America).

You've seen "featureless" landscape. This was "featureful" landscape. Geology having a ball. Tall snow-capped mountains in the distance, seemingly on all points. Meadows, chasms, streams, steep forested hillsides, swampy areas with dead trees, thanks to the impact of beavers.

(Beavers were introduced some time ago and exploded in numbers, having no natural predators.) The guide said that some 80% of the trees are laid low by the wind that prevails there (but we were not experiencing much wind). Saw a large red fox (an introduced animal) and rabbits (an introduced animal). A big condor by a lagoon. A large beautifully-constructed beaver dam. The clouds came and went (mostly cloudy). Water birds were noted by the guide, and their nesting practices, etc., but can't recall the names. Parked 3 times for brief walks. One at the point at which the Pan American Highway ends (begins?), with Alaska on the other end. Floyd and I got our picture taken.

Stopped at a small, well-kept resort building for coffee, tea, juice, snacks, during which a couple staged a stylish (meaning, Argentine-style dress and demeanor) tango dancing.

A word on geography, in case you're interested. Magellan took the first path he encountered when working south along the east coast of South America that would take him (a "first," as we know) from the Atlantic to the Pacific (seeking the spice islands in the Pacific), and it threads along the south end of the continent of South America, beyond which is an archipelago of numerous islands. One major mass of island land is Tierra del Fuego, which was on Magellan's port side. (He saw the night fires lit by natives. He did not know the reason for the fires and thought they were a natural phenomenon. And gave the land its name.) Later, Drake used the same passage but when he reached the Pacific (unlike Magellan, who found a calm ocean), he was greeted by a big storm that blew his ship south and east, through the large (600 north/south miles plus) ocean expanse that separates South America and Antarctica. When weather permitted, Drake resumed his westward course to get to the Pacific, thus "discovering" the passage that bears this name. (Until then, how much "land" lay to the south of the Magellan Strait was unknown.) Later a Dutch ship rounded the southern-most island of the southern archipelago (a few small islands immediately south of Tierra del Fuego) for the first voyage that "rounded" the full extent (islands and all) of the southern end of South America), naming the southern-most one "Hoorn" after the home town of the captain) which gave us the lastingly famous "Cape Horn." And the phrase "rounding the Horn."

The southern region of Chile and Argentina is the Patagonia region. Argentina shrinks down quite a distance short of the southern end of the continent, expanding again to extend into and possess a sizeable triangular-shaped region at the southern end of South America, with the dividing line roughly bisecting Tierra del Fuego. From the Tierra del Fuego National Park it was pointed out that the Chilean line was at the top of a nearby peak. So, much (most) of the southern end of South American is Chilean (to the west, obviously) while Argentina has a section of the east (which undoubtedly has a strange and political explanation that attaches to many demarcations between countries). Ushuaia lies just barely inside Argentina, and offers a good port for the Antarctica trade. By sailing to Antarctica out of Ushuaia, one does not cross the Strait of Magellan (Ushuaia being—if you've paid attention—south of the Magellan Strait). But sailing to Antarctica one crosses, and crosses, and crosses, the Drake Passage, 2 and ½ days, notorious for weather, wind, and rough seas, giving rise to the "Drake" modified phrases, such as "Drake-proofing" your objects in your cabin, the "Drake-walk," etc.

So now I close for the moment, feeling a sense of closure, pointed toward the airports of Santiago, Miami, and Houston, while viewing through the window of my plane out of Ushuaia the utmost beautiful picture of land, sky and lakes—snow-covered peaks of the Andes, spreads of water-lakes, clusters of clouds hovering like mists of guardian angels, pastel colors of blue, white, charcoal and infinity. An awesome lot to have at my back.

ARCTIC

A week's cruise (August 28 – September 4, 2005) of the Arctic Region on Hudson Bay, just south of the Arctic Circle, on board the ship *Ushuaia*, was an eye-opening, information-rich experience. What is the Arctic like? What are its people and cultures and villages like? Animals—marine and land? Birds? Plants and vegetation? Weather? Northern lights? Ice? Seasons? History? Explorations? Northern Passage? Timeline and future?

Amy and I were among 18 passengers on *Ushuaia*. Flew on Air Inuit from Montreal to Kuujjuarapik, a town on the southern part of the western side of the Nunavik Peninsula. Nunavik is a northern region of the Province of Quebec, one of 6 Canadian Provinces (the only French-speaking Province). The Hudson Bay is very large, to the west and north of Nunavik. Our course was to sail north and round the northern end of the peninsula, into the Hudson Strait and southward to the town of Kuujjuaq, a river port, for disembarkation seven days later. Kuujjuarapik is 58° 17' north latitude (077° 43' West longitude). This was the final one of six one-week cruises.[1] Our northern-most latitude was about 62° and some "minutes" (about 30', as I recall from information on the ship's bridge). The Arctic Circle is at approximately 66° north latitude. In the Hudson Bay/Hudson Strait, we were within, say, 100 miles more or less from the Arctic Circle. (Amy and I had crossed the Arctic Circle a few years earlier on a cruise of the Norwegian Fjords, when we flew over the Circle to the start of our cruise at the northern-most reach of Norway, and then we sailed south crossing the Circle again, along the western coast of Norway, resplendent with Fjords.) This fits into the question of "What is the Arctic?" because Norway's climate is significantly influenced by the Gulf Stream, which means that in this region of the "Arctic" there is a milder condition, whereas on the Alaskan/Aleutian side of the Arctic, the "Arctic conditions" extend much further south.[2]

So the "Arctic Region" is not a cleanly defined "circled" area but varies, the Gulf Stream being a major variation factor. (The Arctic Circle is an imaginary line circumscribing the area north of which the sun does not set on the day of the summer solstice [usually June 21] and does not rise on the day of the winter solstice [usually December 21]. At the North Pole, daylight or night lasts up to six months.) If you look down on a globe on the North Pole side, the Arctic Ocean is on top, touching three oceans, Atlantic, Pacific, Indian, but the Arctic is an ice-covered ocean, not a continent. (Antarctica is a snow-covered continent.) Hundreds of miles (varying) south of the North Pole there are islands, etc., through which passage between the Atlantic and Pacific is possible, depending on whether we are talking about small wooden sail ships [17th century, say] or modern ice breakers, as well as whether the season is a cold, icy one, or not (relatively). Typically most of the water in these Arctic Regions is covered with ice during the winter, including large amounts of the Hudson Bay. This is the topic when asking, when, who and how was a Northwest Passage found from Europe (Atlantic) to the Pacific (the spice islands) which was so much sought after, while Magellan was finding such a route to the south of South America (in the 17th century). The Arctic is bordered by Russia's Siberia to the point of the Bering Strait, across which there is Alaska, east of which there is northern Canada and the above-mentioned islands, extending to Greenland, a very large island at the top of the Atlantic.

In Hudson Bay/Hudson Strait, we started in Kuujjuarapik, as stated, in a mild climate, 40s and 50s Fahrenheit during the day, to cold 30s and 40s when we rounded the Nunavik Peninsula.

In flight from Montreal, Martin took the mike and announced that he would video our trip and give everyone a copy (applause). Then each one of us was invited to come forward and speak on the mike (the "phone" that stewardesses use) and say a few words about who we are, why we are making the trip, and how we learned about it (which was videoed). Upon arrival, our de-planing group encountered some 55 passengers who had just disembarked from their week's cruise, now flying back to Montreal. (This Cruise North Expedition is owned by an Inuit-owned corporation which owns, apparently, a number of enterprises related to the region and Inuits. There are 6 one-week cruises in itinerary sets of 2. Ours, the last week, is called "In Hudson's Wake." This is the inaugural season of these cruises, so we are what the U.S. sailors call "original plank holders," meaning the first crew of a new ship.)

At the beginning, let me state some parameters of this account. The Cruise staff provided a very nice end-of-trip re-cap of each day's activities, sightings, flora and fauna, weather, and any significant happenings. This will not be a day-to-day account, but rather an overview and look-back (completed within September, hopefully). A "reflections." You can go deeper by reading the day-to-day account, pictures and related literature.

Generally, the focus was on two things: Arctic conditions (landscape, seasons, animals, etc.) and Eskimos, mainly the Inuits (their history, way of life, present conditions, etc.) (There was little note paid, for examples, to explorations, geology, geography, warming trends, evolution, paleoanthropology—there was not time for "everything." There was a library, and Amy and I took a few books with us based on Cruise North's recommended reading list.) We had landings by Zodiacs—this required boarding of these 6-8 passenger rubber boats down the stairs at the side of the ship and a ride into shore, where disembarking was generally into some shallow water (so we wore rubber boots, and then usually changed to hiking shoes upon reaching beach, and then boots again upon re-boarding the Zodiacs for the trip back to the ship). No docks exist for handling ships, and generally no docks exist. Usually each day we had a landing at a village, and also at a site for walking and looking (tundra, rivers, waterfalls, hills and cliffs). The Zodiac ride could be fraught with spray so we prepared as needed by wearing "shells" (water-proof cover over our trousers) as well as sweaters and windbreakers and, as it got colder, parkas, and as it got even colder, parkas and 2 or 3 sweaters, gloves, headgear).

The *Ushuaia* is a U.S.-built (35 years ago), Panama-registered cruise ship, approximately 300 feet long, capable of 14 knots, 66-passenger capacity, crew of 38, mostly Argentine and the wait staff was mostly Chilean (so Spanish was the operational *lingua franca*). A sleek, blue and white lovely looking ship. (Incidentally, the name is the same as the town on the southern end of Terre Del Fuego, the big island, named by Magellan, on the southern end of South America from which cruise ships ply the Drake Passage across to Antarctica. The *Ushuaia* also does an Antarctic trip during the Antarctic summer [December—February].) It did not have a "new" look. No elevator. Many occasions to climb stairs. Amy and I had an upper-deck "suite," just below the Captain's quarters (on the bridge level) (which gets the full "benefit" when rolling and swaying time comes.) Lounge, bar, dining and library: one deck down. Housekeeping, Zodiac loading, etc.: one more deck down. It was not a luxury ship. But entirely adequate, with good food, good service. It was a cozy ship with a small group that bonded well. No misfits or problem people. An interesting, courteous, supportive group, and diverse. There were a few seniors such as Amy and myself. Excursions were divided into two classes of "challenges" as needed.

There were several village landings. The first village visit, however, was Kuujjuarapik, the village (or town) where our plane landed. Among the villages we saw, there is a high degree of sameness (to us, the passing-through tourists). A landscape of metal buildings (dwellings, co-op, Northern store, administrative building [city hall], school, churches, and a big sports building). We had opportunities to visit inside the administrative building on two occasions, the school on one occasion, the co-op on every occasion (or the Northern store which, I confess, I never got to, although there apparently is a Northern store and co-op in every village). The mayor of two of the villages gave us special attention (remember, this is the first season of this "cruise ship" thing, with tourists coming to gawk and ask questions and—as the villagers are learning—to buy things). The co-op is like any general store in any country town in the U.S., mixed with lots of small grocery stock basics, replete with chips, dips, quick-fix food, junk, junk, junk. This is what they've obtained from advanced societies such as ours. We saw their art to some extent. One co-op had a two-room set up, and we did some looking, handling, and buying, astounded by the prices. One village had a small museum with really nice objects. The art is self-focused on who they are, what they do (hunt), animals that they live with/hunt/kill/eat, artifacts of daily lives. Predominantly soapstone carvings, well done, and other objects made of eclectic materials with excellent craftsmanship. (Is this craft or art? And who's to say?) We had a number of views of displays (at the museum especially) of fur clothing. This has been a really key expertise/know-how that they have developed over 4,000 years. Using the natural resources to clothe and feed and shelter themselves against cold and famine, while maintaining a mobility to follow the seasonal animal movements. Throughout, one theme is prominent: Eskimos have been ingenious, tough, persistent, resilient, to have migrated into this cold arctic country over the Bering Strait 4-5,000 years ago, and to "make it." I will add also: they have lived right down on the land and water, along with the animals, "like" the animals in large measure, living and dying, killing and eating, using sight and smell and instinct and "in-bred" skills, long patience and unstoppable hope.

      Back to the view of the villages. Bleak and barren. Streets are fairly wide, not paved of course. ATV machines (all-terrain-vehicles), like motorcycles except they have four wheels and a small place behind the driver for a passenger (or 2 or 3 or more, depending on children or not, etc.). They were constantly coming and going, leaving trails of dust. Some pick-up trucks. An occasional car. Of course the traffic is light and you can jaywalk with impunity. (Joking, of course—there are no traffic lights or sidewalks.) Usually a police station but not much sign of police. The metal buildings—nothing but metal buildings—set up on pillars about 2-3 feet high. Wondered without finding out about the insulation, the reasons for the fact that the buildings sat off the ground, whether this would be wise in strong winds (but probably snow piles up to building height in the winter), etc. Colors were drab. All in all, the villages were depressing in appearance—little villages populated with "refugee" people from an irretrievably lost culture and way of life with absolutely no visible future.

The people: racially they are of Asian origins. Exactly where is debated and largely lost in antiquity. We have information about the ice ages, the changing levels of the sea which, when "low," exposed the Bering Strait to land crossings for animals and people. There is debate about how many times, and when, but it's generally accepted that there were several (15? 20?) different types of people, even groups that did not survive (some probably left no traces). If glaciers still straddled North America when they came, there was no way to get across, so they made do with what they could find, where there were (in the Arctic). If they could go further south, they become American Indians and later South American Indians. "Eskimos" is the word to overarch the various peoples. Inuits are the large segment in Northern Canada. (Don't rely on this short report: I'm just reciting what I came away with.) In the town of Kuujjuarapik, we learned that there were Cree, Inuits and White. They stubbornly refuse to mix (integrate): separate schools, police force, fire department, etc. And this town has only 1,000 people (more or less—I don't have a record or memory of the number; all of the villages are small: 2-300 in one case, 4-500 in another, etc.).

They never had a written language until it was provided by Edmund Peck (an Englishman, I think) in 1894.[3] So all of their history is oral. They take pride in "stories" of their elders. They are an "elder" respecting people. The elders know how, they know better, you have to mind the elders who make the rules and decide the policies and actions. Amy and I shared a ride in a pick-up truck with a young man (30?) who spoke to this subject, to that effect. Based on what we heard (clearly) from him, there is no wrinkle in this order of things. (As an aside, I asked a young woman at the "reception" desk at the administration building: do you have any lawyers? She spoke English, but she did not know what the word meant! A few other times I used this information to kid about the need for lawyers, or not.)

We asked this young man about whether people "broke the rules" (such as "what rules" were important etc.) and how they were enforced (discipline, punishment). One rule he mentioned, for example, was: if you kill a caribou, you must bring all of it back to the village. (You can't get lazy or whatever and leave some of it "out there.") If you break a rule, then you get the treatment: people "know who you are and what you've done." They shun you for jobs or other privileges. I did not ask if there is a jail, and the answer might well have been negative. At least, in that village. Invariably we encountered a ready warmth, friendliness, openness and helpful attitude. (On one departure occasion, as we boarded the Zodiacs to go back to the ship, Bruce's mother (who lived in that village) appeared with a basket of freshly-picked blueberries to share with all of us. You know that we were touched. (Regarding Bruce, see below.)

Jobs? The only industry is working for the administrative services. Doing administrative work to administer an administration set up to handle the people who do the administrative work. Checks from the Canadian government, presumably. Obviously a few other jobs exist: clerk or manager of the co-op, mayor, policeman, teacher. But there is no industry, no factories. This kind of question was put often, and always the answer was the same.

The old ways. Time and again, everywhere, there is evidence of veneration of, and longing for, the old ways. Living off the land, hunting, following the animal migrations, using the skills and living the life developed over 4,000 years, being like our ancestors. The school we visited had a large class-room exhibit of Inuit artifacts from the old ways. One of our cruse staff members, a woman, who was an Inuit who lived in this area, who had many family members in this area, covered in one of her presentations the need, as she and her parents see it, to keep alive the teaching of the skills of hunting and fishing, of living off the land. She had a word which I did not capture (an Inuit word, of course), that means "eater of raw meat."

She said she is "that," and discussed whether it is derogatory or disparaging. She said she does not deem it to be, but that it is a word to express a simple fact, to denote people who "still" eat raw meat (like her and her ancestors). We asked questions of the mayor, etc., about hunting whales, and quotas. Mayor Andy Moorhouse (village of Inukjuak, Quebec) (who gave us his card) talked about the quota of 15 Belugha whales per village, without regard to its size, and questioned this allotment. (Some Federal governing counsel sets these rules, apparently, consisting of a way to include the native people in the process, apparently.) He said there had been some 6 whales killed so far this season. He talked of sharing (an apparent important characteristic of Inuits), with the elder and handicapped for sure, and maybe with another village, if there's excess or other circumstances. Large extended families are common. One of the mayors (not Moorhouse, who was not asked the question) had something like 64 grandchildren, as I recall.

In addition to the Inuit woman member of the staff mentioned above (Jessie), there was another Inuit, Bruce. Bruce told Amy and me that one of his maternal grandparents and one of his paternal grandparents died of starvation in the 8-year famine circa 1938. I thought: what if I had to say that two of my grandparents died of starvation during a famine? One of our on-board presentations was an old documentary. One part was a man who was Jessie's grandfather. Jessie's grandfather in the film told the story of his grandfather, who was with his mother at a time of famine. They were stranded alone, when she (old at that time) begged him (Jessie's grandfather's grandfather) to kill her and eat her, so that he could have enough strength to get to the place to which they were headed. He (the story-teller) said that he told his mother that he could not do it. She killed herself, and he did take a part of her as food for his journey. He made it, and had children. This was the objective that his mother was pleading for: do this, because there is no other way, and this way you will continue our family line.

And yet, they seem to long for the old way! I wondered on occasion: why did they not go on south in a migration? Seems they could have? But, then, why did Lief Erickson not take his colony on to the south? I wonder. Is it because "they" believed that their "world" was like the rest of the world? Or what?

It seems clear that the old way is gone forever, and that even the Eskimo cultures are gone (going) forever. It is clear that they cannot survive on hunting and fishing. This may be important to them, and it persists to some extent, but it will not sustain them, ever again. Therefore, they must find a future, and at present, there is none. They smoke a lot, even the children. They have a high suicide rate. They have a high school dropout rate. Few go on to college (in Montreal or some other city). During our 30-40 minute session with Mayor Moorhouse (who was jovial, knowledgeable, open, direct, simple, and helpful), there were many questions asked. I asked: do the Inuits have heroes in their stories, legends, myths? (We of the West have Odysseus, Beowulf, Paul Bunyan, King Arthur and the knights, etc., to say nothing of Columbus, Magellan, Drake, Washington, etc.) I was searching for an idea of models to help feed dreams, striving, careers. He seemed to understand my question, and his simple answer was "no." When you are growing up in a dreary Inuit village, what are your models? Personally I had a sense of heartbreak for them. They live on their dreams of the old ways, which have vanished, irretrievably, as I can best see the future of life on earth.

As disclaimers, obviously the places we saw were limited, and our exposure was brief and superficial. Undoubtedly a well-informed person on this subject would find much in this account that could be enlarged, amended or corrected. As tourists/visitors, undoubtedly there was no plan or purpose in giving us lessons on what they were dealing with as "today's" realities, and they probably saw our presence as an occasion to show us the picture of who they are historically (as though, let's say, we were visiting a museum). However, we were there, and this is how it seemed to us, under these circumstances.

Turning now to the nature landings. We saw some scenery sites on brief trips out of the villages: for example, a large and beautiful waterfall, along a stunning river scene, and a few other "great expanse" of low mountains/rolling hills and stretches of tundra. All of this (that is, the landscape we were viewing) is snow-covered in winter. Caribou herds can be found seasonally in the vicinity, which are hunted. Also muskox, polar bears, black bears, arctic fox, lemmings—land animals. Also marine animals: seals, walruses, whales, fish. (Trout. Char [is a kind of staple, and it was served a few times on boar—similar to salmon]. We sighted schools of Char. There were a few fishermen among us, and I did not determine how much success they were having, but we had Char for dinner that night.)

For safety, each group was accompanied by at least one rifle-bearer, in case of a polar bear encounter. Noted is a small rock of an island our zodiacs passed that had dogs, all by themselves. The owner used it as a kennel, collecting the dogs by boat when needed, and feeding them on the island.

To sight the animals is another matter. Here let me make a comparison with Antarctica, to which I traveled in January of last year. In the Arctic, man has had a long presence and he is a very accomplished and feared predator. So the animals keep their distance. You need good binoculars and alertness. ("There, way over there, is a muskox. He's moving over the ridge.") Photos were next to impossible because, say, a muskox would be an unidentifiable dot on the picture. People were constantly saying: look at the ridge over there, then down to your right a little, or such guidances. Binoculars were passed around a little, because some were better than others. Fortunately, my binoculars were pretty good. In its own way, this approach had its interest, and we were all eager participants. In Antarctica, there have been no people (ignoring the recent vintage of some 20 research stations on a huge continent, only some 6 of which remain year-round). In Antarctica, the animals do not fear man. We could walk among colonies of Penguins. Right past pods of seals lolling in piles along the shore. We were required to keep about a 15-foot distance, but sometimes the Penguins forgot the rules and would walk closer by. Generally the animals seemed to totally ignore our presence. In Antarctica we saw lots and lots of animals up close, living their natural activities. Lots of birds, too. In Arctica, there were lots of birds also. Especially migrating geese (saw flocks of snow geese and Canadian geese, resting on the ground, flying past).

Viewing a nesting colony of thick-billed Murres on the high vertical cliffside of Diggs Island deserves some special report. The bird is large, 1-2 feet (?). Black on top, white underneath (reminded me of Penguins, only smaller). At peak population, there are some 30,000 pairs nesting there (the third largest nesting colony for Murres on earth). We were not at the peak time, but there were large numbers. The chick is born relatively late in the summer season. Develops very large black feet, for a reason. Male and female parents alternate feeding chores. The egg is constructed so that if it is "knocked" it tends to spin (and not roll like a regular egg tends to do), so that it is less likely to fall off the sparse cliff-side nesting place. Even before the chick can fly it is pushed out of the nest, to glide with its under-formed wings to a "landing" on the cold water hundreds of feed below. The male parent and chick then begin a 1,000-kilometer swim to the winter grounds, during which the "father" teaches the chick to feed. Feeding is by diving. It does not involve spotting the prey, then diving for it. It involves becoming fish-like and swimming under water in search of food. So the big feet are what the chick needs, and flying can come later (and is achieved by the end of the journey, when it graduates). I asked the naturalist (Teresa, a lovely young woman with knowledge and conscientious helpfulness) "why" this biology plan. She did not have an explanation. At the re-cap session on board at 6:30 (a regular routine for each staff naturalist and participant to report and discuss the events of the day) she assigned the question to the passengers. Next day I proposed: the hatching is late, learning to fly takes time, big feet will do the trick for their type of feeding (to swim fast under water), they've got a thousand kilometers to cover, learning to feed does not involve "flying," so all that's needed can be accomplish while getting on with the imperative business of going south "on time."

Diggs Island. As stated, very high, sheer cliffs. We landed at the base of a draw, which extended steeply over boulders, choppy ground, etc., to a top with marvelous views. (The ship was a small vessel out there, Zodiacs below were little boats hurrying along.) For the landing the group was divided into climbers and birders. The latter were treated to Zodiac rides along the base of the cliff to see the birds on the cliff and birds skimming the water in small covies, while bouncing along in a bowl of weather and beauty. (Fortunately, the climbers got a brief excursion along the cliff base for viewing the Murres, because we could not see them from the top.)

You had to sign up the night before for the climb. I had failed to sign up, so while preparing for the Zodiac departures I asked Brad, the senior staff person, if I could go with the climbers. He said, well, yes, but I need to point out that the climb will be very challenging. I said, well, I think you can make it, Brad, so I hope you will come too.

I was aware of the fact that that day, Thursday, September 1, was my birthday (74th), but it had not been much on my mind. Until I was near the top of the climb, huffing and puffing, I'll admit (although, so were the other 8 or 10), when I had this thought: what a birthday! First, thankfully I'm physically able to do this. Second, it's such a special place to be, thing to do. How lucky I am, here in the Arctic, climbing a natural wonder, viewing the top of the world from a topped-up place, with companions sharing an experience worthy of cherishing. (That evening, Amy had arranged, and as dinner closed, to my complete surprise, a birthday cake with candles was brought in by chef and staff. Happy birthday song by everyone. A card (selected by Linda in an Inuit village the day before) which she arranged to have signed by all. The Captain joined the dinner for the occasion. Pictures and a speech. (Yes, it was short, and buoyed by 2 glasses of wine.) I just had to tell you about this birthday experience.

The tundra is a special land. We were above the tree line by far (except at the very beginning and ending of our cruise). Not a tree or shrub to be seen anywhere (a lamentable absence for people who live among and love trees). Ground covered by moss and lichen. Frequent patches of flowering plants, tiny, ground-hugging, existence-hugging, beautiful (more so because they were tiny and seemed so precarious). Red, green. Many rocks, many kinds, shapes, colors—holding the secrets of eons of plate tectonics, weather, crust erosions, re-cycling, freezing and thawing. Permafrost underneath. Nothing could afford to send roots to the permafrost. The soil was soft but poor (although, misleadingly, it "looked" rich). Many water scenes—rivers, lakes, ponds (some freeze all the way to the bottom), and, of course, the vast Hudson Bay.

I've heard "tundra" many times. Now I have a deeper concept of "tundra." At first it seemed to be a barren expanse of wasteland. As I paid more attention, to the land and what the naturalists were pointing out, I saw a richness of life. A special life adapted to survival in a harsh and frigid place of existence-striving. Another way to see life as a miracle. It has a beauty, a music, a proclamation, a yearning to go on, forever. I'm so glad I saw it, this barren tundra.

Often saw rocks stacked in "design" format, indicating or signifying something. As I understand it, if the rock formations have "sculpture" intentions, such as a representation of a human form, the Inuit name is, I think, *Inuksuit*. There are also "cairns" (if I use this word correctly) which are utilitarian stacks or formations of stones. (Travelers or explorers placed notes [information], as well as supplies, in such stone caches.) One very tall one (over 8 feet) was probably a landmark or reference point for land "navigation." We had asked Mayor Moorhouse what these rock formations stood for (and the concept was "general"). He said several things and added: some of them may be just a statement: "Johnny was here." A key use of piling stones was to stash excess food for a later day, to keep bears and foxes from taking it, so you could see that it had a "hollow" inside. On Diane Island we came upon a burial area. Graves delineated by stones piled in a grave-like form (another use). One stack of stones was a different approach. It was about 3-4 feet at the base, and about 5 feet high. It contained human bones, which could be viewed by peering through the openings between the stones. A way to bury a body and protect it from animals.

We did not spot any whales, although a sighting of whales is usually likely. Belugha is the most likely. A very large whale. The Belugha, Bowhead and Narwhal are the only three truly Arctic whales (remaining there all year). A distinguishing characteristic is that these whales have no dorsal fins; apparently this avoids contact and friction with the ice "above" them. They can break through the ice, depending on its thickness and which whale, of course. The names are not uniformly spelled and the names may be sometimes associated with a different fish or whale, depending on which country or language, etc. The Orca visits the region in the summer months, but does not stay year-round. The Narwhal has a long spear (the outgrowth of a tooth) protruding from its head, usually a single one on its left side (rarely two) ranging up to 4-6 feet in length and is usually only a male characteristic. You can find discussions linking this animal to the stories and myths of unicorns.

We saw polar bears! On a day after we weathered a storm, we were taking shelter behind (leeward side, between the island and the mainland) Akpatok Island (on Saturday, at the end of which we would sail the 10-hour home stretch overnight to Kuujjuaq, needing to time the arrival to be at high tide so we could enter the port on the inland side of the river mouth), we saw bears, and were positioned on the ship to see them fairly well (through binoculars, mainly from the bridge). About 10, here and there (some said 14). We had planned to make a landing on Akpatok Island but the weather was still rough, so the landings were cancelled. A day on the ship, which seemed all right after the night we had experienced. Also, I wondered (and never asked or found out), how could we have landed on this island with bears all around? I suspect that we could not have, for the reason of bears alone. Apart from this sighting, we did not see any polar bears. By the way, during nature landings, there were always 2 guides with rifles. You had to stay in close groups, not go wondering off. It was possible to split into two groups (1 rifle bearer each), for those who wanted to venture to an in-land, or high-up, hike, and a group for those who wanted to putter around near the landing spot. (In fact on one occasion when Amy was hanging back near the shore, she had the company of two rifle-bearing protectors.) A polar bear can appear suddenly from over the ridge, even pop up out of the water. (The cruise immediately before us had the experience of a polar bear showing up near the beach; that group had to take to the Zodiacs. There is a connection among guides by walkie-talkie, so the inland group was warned, etc.)

It was a dark and stormy night! I'm referring to a storm that rocked the ship between, say, 7:30 p.m. to 11:30 p. m. on Friday, September 2. Some said it was effects from Hurricane Katrina that still had some life as it traveled northward near Greenland (to the east of us, without much land-break between whatever was "out there" and our little ship sailing from Diane Island to Akpatok Island), the same hurricane that had devastated New Orleans (a disaster that we were to learn about at the end of the cruise). We had had a marvelous nature landing on Diane Island. The seas had become a little rough, causing some seasickness among the landlubbers. But we quickly developed our sea-legs and got along fairly well through dinner. We had been "advised" of rougher weather coming our way. Various strategies were adopted to handle the blow. Amy and I chose to go to bed. Our suite was on an upper, forward deck (worst place to be when the ship does its thing, except maybe where the Captain was).

As I mentioned, our suite was directly under the Captain's quarters. Anything not tied down went aflying when the ship took a surge, a roll, a rock-back, a "completion" roll the other way. Play that again, time after time. We were literally holding on to our beds, else we would have become one of those flying things. Above us we heard what sounded like furniture careening across the floor as the ship took some major rolls. (The Captain didn't nail down his stuff?) I "calculated" with great care on some of the rolls: 45° at least. (An interesting process, to judge from a bed the swings and swells and falls and swings, how much is the rolling of the ship.) In the darkness, a few hours later, Amy and I said aloud: is there seriously a risk that this may not work? I played through some thoughts of where the life jackets were, where we would go, etc., but I didn't want to sound alarmed. I was not ever "really" alarmed, but, but, this rocking and rolling and pitching kept on keeping on. When a big roll happened, and we were at its "bottom," I thought: come on ship, come on back up.

Amy has carried the belief about herself that she's prone to seasickness. No more. She never got sick! I have carried the belief that I never get seasick, and I've sailed on small boats many times, overnight into the Gulf, etc., and I've crossed the Drake. However, at the beginning of that day I had a brief moment. Fortunately it passed in minutes. At about 11:30 I went to the lounge area (one deck down) and found a number of fellow passengers using the floor for sleeping, with chair and couch cushions strewn about, "etc." They said that the stern deck on the other side of the glass wall had wondrous scenes of seas bowling over the sides. The ship settled down. (I suppose this was the time of crossing into the leeward side of Akpatok Island.) Later the Captain told me that the rolls had reached 25° (by his instruments, I suppose) and—reassuringly- he said the Ushuaia can take a roll up to 60°. Shucks. We could have had more!

On the day of the big rolls, but before we got into the worst of it, we had the Captain's Dinner. Complete with the Captain, his first mate (a woman) and the Ship's doctor—in their white, epaulettes-adorned traditional dress. Our Captain was a delightful Argentine, and always open and friendly on the bridge (except the bridge was closed during heavy seas). I was on the bridge when we entered the river-port of Kuujjuaq, where the earlier cruise got on the sandbar, and the Captain was "pre-occupied" during this stretch. The dinner was very enjoyable, with enough toasts to go around. I later wondered: he planned it so we would have the Captain's dinner before hitting the rough weather! (Just joking, I think.)

We had daily presentations in the "Conference Room" of documentary films and talks by naturalists with slides. And Martin gave us occasional installments of what he had videoed so far. We held one lounge room session of Inuit "games" presented and demonstrated by Bruce and Jessie. Feats of balance and kick. After some of them, we were invited to try it. Kelly tried almost every one. I did two. (Need I tell you: with great success of course, as I tell this story.) Martin also took some turns. The documentaries were vintage "old" but starkly authentic, showing how the Eskimos lived, worked, and played. Talks on whales, birds, wild plants. Well selected and presented, and, of course, very informative about where we were.

Northern Lights! Also known as the aurora borealis. They appeared at 10 or so each evening, and especially at 11, 12 or so, according to reports. Amy and I were missing them at first because of bedtime. One night Martin did us the favor of knocking on our door (as pre-arranged) and we went outside. Wow is what I said. Beautiful, ephemeral, gossamer, luminous, mysterious, ghostly, other-worldly, beautiful, changing before the eyes, streaks and colors, like a message or sign from some great being or place, dancing, beautiful. I began to think: somewhere down here is a small ship, with some small people, on a giant planet, inching along the arctic waters, looking skyward, in awe. I hugged my wife.

I was eager to see the starry night sky. I wish I could report great success. Sky plastered with bright dots. I did see "some" of this, and I'm sure that others saw more. I did not get a full load. I wanted to identify the North Star (Polaris). I think I did. At the North Pole, of course, it is directly overhead, and never moves. All other stars and planets revolve around it. A pure happenstance of the construction of the universe, and our place in it. There is no comparable star for the Southern Hemisphere. (It is the star by which sailors know their latitude in the Northern Hemisphere. [It's so easy I've always said that there's not a sailor with a bad latitude.] Longitude has been a different matter, in the extreme, historically.) I certify to myself that it's found by following the two exterior stars on the cup of the Big Dipper, and following a projected straight line to Polaris.

Reflections miscellany:

It was indeed a worthwhile experience. Mind and awareness expanding. I had a special reason to appreciate the journey, having traveled, as stated, to Antarctica last year. (There were two other passengers [to my knowledge] who also had been to Antarctica.) My interest is to learn and try to absorb more about the planet we inhabit: such trips add information to questions such as: what is it, its history, its future, its people? And this adds to "what's a planet?" in this universe. What's its timeline, place? And on and on.

The group of us seemed to bond exceedingly well. Everyone had something to contribute. Relationships were always courteous, open, supportive. Humor was abundant. The staff was unfailingly courteous and helpful, and they seemed to have the knowledge for the occasion. Brad, the chief of staff, had many years of experience on expeditions from Egypt to Antarctica to Arctica to probably anywhere you care to name. We saw no tensions or moments. This account does not attempt to cover all individuals by name and characteristics. Likewise I have not attempted to mention and identify all of the passengers. Kelly worked for the Massachusetts Audubon Society. Merv and Linda operate expeditions from Winnipeg to Churchill (the town near the western shore of Hudson Bay) where Polar Bears gather each year during a brief period before heading out on the ice to hunt for seals. Two passengers, Nancy and Nancy, had been on an earlier cruise that ran aground on a sandbar on the first day of sailing forth, and remained on board for 3 days before being "evacuated." The ship was inspected for hull damage by divers and the captain was replaced. Martin came with his father, Ray, whose other son, Peter, was the chef on the cruise (and, saying it again, the food was good). I don't know where to stop. We got to know each other's brief profiles and to build brief, enjoyable friendships.

I'm sure each passenger's account would have different "takes" on what the experience was. In a way, I'm reminded of the two blind men feeling the parts of an elephant and expressing their respective views of what the animal was. Where do you "come from"? What were you paying attention to on the trip? What's your world view? My front-and-center experiences were, to see "it," to fit it into my conception of our planet, to compare it to Antarctica, to know more about the animals and all of the flora and fauna that belong to the Arctic, and to "see" the people and their culture. I was pleased and satisfied, except, I have to say, the Inuits (and by extension, the Eskimos) left me with a feeling of sadness and anxiety for them.

Human dreams of, and passions for, reaching the poles have been fuel for mankind's indomitable spirit for "questing" that has written exciting histories of high adventures of discovery. There are two "poles," each one marking the extreme "ends of the earth" characterized by special and extreme frigid conditions and "life"—and this happens because of the way the earth "presents itself" to the sun during its daily rotations and annual orbits. "Ice ages" also come and go across eons of time because of the vacillations of the earth's "tilt" relative to the sun. The "pole" in each case is not a precise, immovable location (and "where" it is depends, for example, on whether you mean the magnetic pole or the geographic pole). You don't have to fulfill a journey to the poles themselves to gain a view and some knowledge of the Polar Regions. In the case of Antarctica it was (for me) the Peninsula and its waters and islands; for Arctica, it was Hudson Bay and its waters and islands. There are other routes to take, other places to go, for experiencing a presence in the Polar Regions. My mind is not free from thoughts and wishes for more. But I find satisfaction in having experienced a presence in the Polar Regions of our earth, and thereby to augment my knowledge of who we are.

I'm also sort of sad that there are only two poles.

PERU, AMAZON, CUSCO

Thursday, February 18[4]

Peru is larger than life. The Andes—like a backbone, majestic, running the full length, and on into Chile and southward nearing the tip of South America before it dives underground. The Amazon Basin, where the feeder-tributaries in this massively-large rain-forest basin gather with cornucopian potency to produce that very long and very large river that conjures so much—the Amazon—a huge river for sure with boggling data scales. The Amazon Basin has rain forests, flora and fauna in varieties and splendor beyond imagination. The desert-dry elongated ocean-hugging seam of coastal land with Andean-fed rivers crossing the dry land with stretches of oasis-fertility. Civilizations that have come and gone, leaving vapor trails of mystery, peopled by raw basic human grist, splendid works of man in ceramic, stone, metal and textile art, thriving skills and imaginations that blossomed across the regions of every kind, and more. All of this ancient enduring wonder now being pushed inexorably upon the shores of a modern world. If you were headed toward this place, what would your expectations be, without even asking why would you go?

So here I am, on a plane from Houston to Lima, February 18, 2010, to link with a group to tour the Amazon Basin rivers and rain forests in the area near Iquitos and Nauta. Nine days on a river boat, excursions on skiffs and canoes for sighting birds, animals, scenery; a side venture to a village by skiffs; natives and Shamen; fish and birds, and our cousin primates still doing what we used to do. After the Amazon, a portion of the group will go to Cusco, 11,000 feet high in the Andes, the ancient capital of the Inca Empire, and tour the Sacred Valley through which flows from these lofty heights the Urubamba River on a journey to Machu Picchu. Our trip, originally scheduled to visit Machu Picchu, will stop short of this promised land because heavy rains and resulting mud slides have wiped away a portion of the train tracks needed for getting there. A bummer, but a fact.

I'm reading *Frommer's Guide of Peru*, skimming, realizing how woefully much I don't know, how big the destinations will be and wondering why I did not do more preparation. I realize now—begin to realize now—how vast and full the scene will be—the little taste of Peru that I will have.

The Amazon has been high on my list of must-visit places because, I think, of all of the grand images such as I mentioned above. Who would not want to visit the Amazon? And the grand Inca civilization. It took me 78 years to make the move. Now I'm headed to Lima, scheduled to arrive at 1130p.

The plane arrives at 1145 p. For one hour I go step by slow step through immigration and customs. Silent people processing—check and look and guard—thinking of all the airport security clearing at the boarding point—shoes off, pockets emptied, scanning, guards watching, thinking of the waste of much of what we are, or what we would like to be, a soft brutalizing of our self-civilizing social evolution. With no incidents, I pass through the sieve of the Lima airport.

The exit from customs is into a sea of waiting people greeting people. The people on the plane, in the immigration line, the exit sea people, present for me a "different look." This is Peru, with Peruvian faces and features, land of ancient cultures, indigenous Indians, propagations through the ages of battles and strifes, work and love, learning and doing what life on earth requires.

In the greeting sea, an array of names on placards are held up. I scan name after name hoping to find me, and do.

His name, like mine, is William. I had the thought: a Lima limo. But a limo it was not. A small stick shift less-than-new car of a make not apparent to me. William's *poquito* English, and pronunciation

thereof, and my hearing deficit, invited a fair amount of re-runs. My Spanish was impeccable and fluent, of course, as long as we stayed with the "me Tarzan" range.

Between midnight and one a.m. our small box on wheels rolled along the streets of one- and two-story buildings that were mostly dark but for mild street-lighting. They even seemed unused, stacked and stuck together in continuous box-lines and variegated materials, windows, ledges, roofs, and significations of the absence of prosperity. At one intersection when stopped for a red light, a small boy—was he 8 or 12 or 14?—stepped in front of our car, holding three 18" sticks, each tipped with a vibrant ball of flame. There, like an impromptu magician our of the city's dark hat, he performed a juggling artistry of dazzling sticks-on-fire from the arms and hands of a small Lima-boy-wanting-money. I made use of the *cambio* that I had just received at the airport, my hand to his through the car window, lowered by William's touch of a button, that for a flickering moment drew aside the curtain between me and this boy-child of the dark 1 a.m. Lima street.

I checked into the Sonesta El Olivar Hotel in a very late at night, one-clerk-one-porter dim-light feeling. The hotel's name signifies its location on the edge of a park that is an olive grove, not visible until morning. Thus I begin my arrival in Lima by going to sleep.

Friday, February 19

I awake at 630. My hotel room is 3 rooms, counting the commodious marbled bathroom as one, it's so large—and everything, except the ceiling, in light earthen-brown, rich white-veined marble. Living room, bedroom, balcony overlooking (2nd floor) the tops of olive trees and morning walkers, and one talkative dove. The bathroom has a jacuzzi, a sauna, a large totally marbled shower stall, a separate large marbled room for side-by-side douche and toilet bowls and in the main part a long marbled shelf with sinks backed by an ample mirror-mirror on the wall.

Looking at the craftsmanship of the marble work I thought of the Inca masonry skills that I've been reading about. This is a Holiday Inn version of Machu Picchu, not likely to last out the centuries, but pleasant to the pass-this-way-once-in-a-lifetime tourist I am. (Actually a first class hotel, but I like saying it that way.)

Breakfast on the ground floor restaurant busy with what seemed like business types, mostly men. Pleasant buffet, but Paris it is not.

In my room I receive the 9a call that my driver is here, as arranged. His name is Carlos, sporting a nice up-to-date car. In *un poquito* English he asks, as we drive away, what address? I say, pull over and let's talk about our choices. Quickly it becomes apparent he is not a guide as I had specified in several pre-arrival emails with Elvira when the topic of what I wanted to see was being covered, and I had a choice of a driver or a driver/guide. So, back to the hotel to try to fix this problem. Carlos on the Spanish phone, talking and talking. Then he says to me, the guide will be here in 10 minutes. Sure, I say to myself. In 10 minutes another car and driver appear—Rafael. He is a guide, and we proceed.

The first destination is the Museo Larco. It is stunning—no exaggeration. As one nears the entrance, there is a lovely landscape of structures and rows of blossoming flowers of vibrant colors. A warm inviting setting, lightly peopled. I ask Rafael if he wants to go with me, as he seems to want, so I buy 2 tickets. I like this decision, having as companion a local Limagian (I wonder what the correct word is?), and harboring the thought, as wrong as it is, that I have in tow a native who is hundreds of years old, as we begin our tour of Peruvian history showcased by extraordinary pre-Columbian art. I have viewed pre-Columbian art on a number of occasions, but this one is captivating.

There are artifacts from various cultures, spanning 5,000 years. For whatever reasons, I was not expecting what I was seeing. Ceramics, stone, metal, textiles—on and on—displayed in clean lines and light and space, in rooms of architectural tastefulness of design and material—quiet, blending, but rich and right. The artifacts are mind-bending assimilations of disparate images, concepts, colors, material—brilliant piece after brilliant piece. I recall that when I saw the Lascaut cave paintings I knew Picasso had been there (and, as I learned later, he had indeed). I'm thinking Picasso did not see this, and if he had, he may have gone back to school. Imagination on a spree of fantasizing but holding together harmony and sense—sense out of nonsense—nonsense and impossible images pooling into a work to be right and beautiful and utterly arresting. Time and cultures parade as we walk room by room—an hour and a half of this genius of Peruvian artistry roaming across centuries, right into my eyes and brain.

Now and then Rafael and I make comments to each other, in part to express our wow. (There is only one other person, in another room.) It is a delightful way to begin my one-day tour of Lima. However—yes, however—at one wall there are images and descriptions of the religious practices focused on human sacrifice. It chills the soul. I decide then and there that I will re-do the history of mankind to wipe away all of his evil, brutality, even his unkindnesses, so that our history pours forth only our good and beautiful—nothing else. I then decide to set about re-doing our present and our future as well. Why didn't someone else think of this, long ago? How it needs to be done! And the question/wish: can we, and maybe . . . .

As we left there was a side section displaying a large amount of Peruvian erotica ceramics. (Reminded me of the Chinese school of this type. I think there is a name for this motif but I don't recall.) In any case, the somewhat extensive display of ceramic figures in various coupling modes clearly shows with complete and bold frankness that the ancient Peruvians also knew about sexy sex.

Well, it's 1115 and time to drive a short distance to the city's coast-edge, to the Pacific, to the restaurant I've read about and it dovetails with Rafael's recommendation: Costa Verde. A nice drive along the beach line of surfers and beach people at the wave-edge of the peaceful blue Pacific. At one section the traffic got slow and Rafael explained that they are adding land to this area, pointing out the trucks arriving with their loads of soil. Making Peru bigger, apparently. I asked him if the plan was to build more Andes-by-the-sea. At least he laughed.

Costa Verde. Beautifully appointed entrance and restaurant, going past a lovely bar (led on by a lovely hostess), display of buffet preparation. This restaurant is famous for its seafood buffet, featuring ceviche (as many Lima restaurants do), in a quasi-outside enclosure of tables looking out onto a scene of jetty, shored up by big rocks, a beach, ocean and mountainsides in the view. It is big and empty except for one other table (and they leave soon, leaving me as the sole customer with an over-ample supply of waiters). (Note: as I suspected, noon is not lunch time in this San Isidor District of Lima—as I leave at 130, the restaurant is beginning to fill, but meanwhile I relish.) I decide not to invite Rafael to lunch with me and to enjoy a quiet beautiful feast alone.

I start with a Pisco Sour, as delicious a drink as I've ever had. Not made like the Pisco Sour of Santiago where I first had Pisco Sour a few years ago. This one is a superior cousin to the Ramos Gin Fizz of Brennan fame. Frothy like ambrosia. After the first sip it purrs continuously.

My waiter is avuncular, and often stands nearby just minding his business of minding me. He goes with me to the buffet, urging this and that—an excess of delectable concoctions of seafood appetizers—choose-what-you-want dishes, and you want everything. After settling on a plate of beautiful things, and another Pisco Sour, *Tio* Julian on his own initiative brings some extras, things that I obviously should have chosen so he chose for me. One is fried calamari and sauce that shame, and will forever shame, all other presentations thereof. How I wish I had remembered to bring with me my 3 other stomachs!

Ceviche is their game in Lima, and Costa Verde is on top of this game. *Tio* Julian said that I should let him fetch my ceviche and I do. A sea-bass-based plate of superlative delectables. I would describe its details but I would fail. Of course I think of Amy and how much she would have enjoyed being here, and I having her here.

Finishing that, *Tio* Julian says something I cannot de-code, so he asks me to follow him, which I do, to the buffet zone. He shows me a table (3 or 4) of what must be the main course choices. But I have to say *lo siento, no mas.* Then he walks me past the desserts. *Lo siento, no mas, no mas.*

It ends with coffee and a last savor of Magellan's Pacific Ocean.

By the way, it costs $40—not including tip, which I am asked to hand to *Tio* in cash, which I do. $40 never had a better ride.

Rafael is waiting. We do the brief coastal road to downtown (near Lima Centro, to which I am not going today, saving it for the group trip tomorrow) to the Museo Nacion. I will speak of sdriving about the city. Rafael is a good driver, and pleasant company/information. The traffic is not bad and drivers are courteous and move along, elbowing into lanes and accepting of one another. The line of buildings consists of mostly 2-story heights with pockets of multi-story (more than 2) buildings. Unlike the night-time view when driving from the airport, in daylight the buildings sport a lot of color—ochre, green, yellow, earthy-brown—on and on. Instead of free-standing (many are, of course), the structures are joined as though long rows of townhouses except these are stores and offices. The flora has the equatorial range although the coastal area is relatively dry. (The Andes and Pacific collaborate to create a multi-faceted geology and weather.) Many parks. Trees include fascinating trunks of aged, gnarled and knobby bodies, with twisting, often spiraling, lines. (Later in the day, at twilight, I walk a good distance, but not the full length, of the olive grove park at the hotel, a beautiful population of old and gnarled-body trees, enjoyed by a relatively sparse cast of all ages, the world pleased and at ease with itself.) Our trips to and fro the coast (a late afternoon one to come) are short. I enjoy the driving around and the logistics do not require too much of this. A fair amount of road work signs of a city with normal healthy growing pains.

The Museo Nacion building itself stands out as we approach. Quite tall (6 stories) with a solid towering block feel, dark bown/gray stone look. Both outside and inside, the eyes are invited to scan upward, to feel uplifted. Part of the exhibit is closed (remodeling) but there are several areas of archeological artifacts of beauty. An extensive display of ceramics of bulls of various sizes. (I'm recalling the Hall of the Bulls in Lascaut) They are astonishing—color, design, imagination, artistic freedom and range. I ask Rafael, why no horse, not at all, here (so far) or at Museo Larco, even though some of the art was post-Columbian? He says maybe the Peruvians did not want to incorporate what the Spanish brought, wanted instead to stick with what was theirs. (I recall reading recently about the first encounter the North American Southwest Indians had with the horse that the Spanish brought and how awed they were. So I was puzzled. Turns out, the next room had some good horse pieces in the mix.) Of course, the many presentations of the bull needs understanding and discussion, as well as more time to write about it, and I don't have much of any of that. I do report that I continued to be excited by the originality and imagination speaking out so loudly. This is true throughout the many presentations of bulls. Adorned, colorful, big bodies, expressive facial features. Often the back of the bulls have opening spouts and curved handles, because, as I understand it, these were vessels for liquids, used for drinking. This was a typical configuration. And finally I saw horses, statuesque Chinese style.

A decision. On the sixth floor there is an exhibit of the Shining Path episode that reached a zenith of terrorism in Peru some 20 years ago—a Marxist organization committed to violence, brutality, bloodshed, hostages, etc. We take the elevator but then I prefer to make a short work of it. Big sprawling photos of dead people in the street, etc. Their thinking, it seems, is that this episode is a part of Peruvian history so let it exhibit. I am deeply conflicted, as I am seeing so much in life that is cruelty. I think of man's inhumanity to man and wonder why we use the "in" before "human?" Man's brand of humanity, the "humanness" of us, is what's going on.

Now I'm seeking contemporary Peruvian art. We drive to the Lima Museum of Art (exact name?), a large building located in a campus-like area of interesting "museum" buildings nestled within very busy streets. But unfortunately it is closed. (Rafael says he had called in advance and was told it was open—entirely likely based on my shallow experience with the spotty reliability of information.) This building is one of several in the grassy groves, trees, imaginative architecture, park-like area. We went across a complex of expansive web of streets to the Italian museum. Very typical Italian paintings and sculpture—and interesting for a brief visit.

Next, and last for the day, at Rafael's suggestion we drive back to the coast to visit Barrando, an artist colony by the sea. Good streets of cobblestone, rows of apartments or houses, shops and restaurants, some bohemian flavor, here and there are stalls to sell curios. A good cobblestone street-end that meets the Pacific, with a view along the coast. I bought a CD of Andesean instrumental music from a 2-piece performing band. This area is very pleasant and inviting, but light is fading and we have to go. At the hotel I settle up with Rafael in accordance with the pre-arrangement, with a tip of course. I had learned a little about Rafael's family, enjoyed the day with him and his helpfulness, and thus it was a fleeting meet-and-part with a friend . When has anyone done this before?

As mentioned above I have a nice twilight walk in the Olive Grove, have a small dinner at the hotel, and to bed.

Saturday, February 20

At breakfast I spot a couple at a table who are wearing the Harvard name badge so I say hello, and after going through the buffet line I join them. This is the gathering of the group, to get ready to depart.

We leave hotel Sonesta el Olivar by bus to visit the Plaza de Armes, a large "el centro" park occupying a full, large block. We first visit the San Francisco Monastery, and then walk to the Cathedral to experience the ecclesiastical and oldness of Lima. I will move on now because of my feeling that old cathedrals are much like old cathedrals, with just a few general observations. The monastery was built (and built and built) starting in 1535 by the Catholic Church that swept in behind Pizarro's overpowering entrance on the Inca stage in 1532. The conquering and subjugating of Inca Peru was done quickly, took only a few years to consolidate, done by a force of only some 300 soldiers (initially) in face of what must have been thousands and thousands of Inca warriors.

Pizarro's arrival by happenstance was at the end of a devastating seven-year civil war (2 Inca leader-brothers fell out), and somewhere in this time line a devastating plague of some European disease (probably smallpox) had made its way to Peru from the European landings on the east coast. So the mighty Inca Empire had come, by its own doing and the plague, to its knees. Every conquistador should have it so lucky. Pizarro, a young conquistador, was assassinated in 1542. The frescos, architecture and artistic adornments of the Monastery brought Spain to Lima. A lot of Moorish design was evident (Moorishness was at that time also a part of Spain). We did 15 minutes in the catacombs, consisting of tunneling and tombs. It is interesting that this huge Cathedral structure has withstood the many earthquakes that like to shake and rumble Peruvian landscapes, often with disastrous ramifications. The large columns have an interior matting and netting material—as opposed to solidity—that absorbs shocks. The flat ceilings of the catacombs are flat brickwork with the question: what keeps them from falling? Answer: the cement is a mix of unusual things (including guano and egg white) and has done a superb job of staying put.

The walk-about touring ended at Casa Aliago, a large (66 rooms) private residence of great importance, dating back to Pizarro's days, built by one of his officers, and it is still in the same family (17 generations). The *grande dame* is 92 years old and lives here (although I note that she did not greet us). The rooms are treasures, containing treasures. We are greeted (instead) by a small staff of "uniformed" waiters and a resident guide who shows us and talks some of what we are seeing. Then wine, soft drinks, pisco sours, a chocolate-like pisco drink which I sampled, and more pisco sour, as well as a well-done series of hors d'oeuvres. Then lunch around a long (need I say) old table, good food, beautifully served.

When you go to Lima and wonder where to stay, I recommend Casa Aliago.

    To the bus, to the airport, 3-hour flight to Iquitos. I could take the time and space to describe in detail the airports and airplane, luggage handling, announcements, etc., but you'll forgive me if I just turn to the Iquitos page.

    Iquitos arrival is at dusk. The town seems like a house that Jack built, which one would expect. A sense of sprawling neighborhoods and streets meandering about the area, getting denser as we approach the center. Hotel El Dorado faces onto a lovely square/park with a tall central monument honoring somebody, and 4 tall flag poles. The staff behind the desk is one person, so a little effort and patience are required, and well observed. We meet again in the lobby in short order for a bus to a spot for boarding, in very dim light and tricky footing, a boat for a short ride to a floating restaurant—all in the midst of not a lot of light. All of us quietly purring along dark water with lights to see "out there" from unknown situations, coming to the dock of a floating building. Almost spooky. The 2-story boat/restaurant has ample staff, friendly, helpful. A long table between the open-air exterior walls and a square of counters that section off a central open kitchen, populated by 6 or 7 chef-attired young men. The food and drink convey the message that this is Peruvian regional cuisine, a lot of seafood choices and sauces that required a lot of discussion with the waiters, resulting in lingering uncertainty. Everybody seemed to get away pleased, as we boated and bussed ourselves back to Hotel El Dorado for the night.

Sunday, February 21

    I am up early for breakfast and a walk in the park/square that the hotel faces onto. Another Plaza de Armes neatly patterned to fold inward to a monolith monument, apparently with military significance.

    On the other side is a very picturesque church (cathedral?) in yellow and maroon, with a sky-reaching façade and high, big entrance opening. I take some pictures, walk around. I notice a slow, gradual gathering of dressy military types. As time slowly passes, more and more, indicating different branches because of different styles and colors. Definiely a "parade" dress and not a crack-heads moment. A flag brigade of 5 young soldiers stand stiffly with folded flags at the base of two slender, very tall flag poles. (As time passes, these soldiers have the role of holding this pose for, it seems, at least an hour and a half, waiting for the picture and management to compose itself into a state of readiness, with an excruciatingly this-will-never-really-happen sense of mañana.)

Apparently this Sunday morning has some kind of significance so the military is putting on a dressy show, with little groups of lined-up soldiers (young men and women, really young), whose uniforms just came off the shelves of new and neat. I have no information access to understand the occasion, but this does not matter—it's the scene. At one point I go over to the church and step inside, where service is in progress, with a short supply of people clustered near the front of a (of course) very large, ornate interior, etc. Quite a lot of people in and around the square and church, with no cars (traffic is cordoned off), and overlaid by a quietness as though seen from some far-away perspective. How many times and places is this scene happening? At the entrance of our hotel several people (a few of our group) are gathered to be onlookers, and 4 or 5 young boys hang around trying to sell us things, more pleasant than annoying, wearing T-shirts with American-style wordings. And the band plays on.

Left the hotel at about 9a (and had to walk around the corner and down the street because the bus had been cordoned off and could not approach the hotel). An old bus, described below. Drive through parts of Iquitos to see vegetable market, flower market, parks and Iquitos scenes including the bordering river views (not the Amazon, though it is nearby).

The streets are filled with rickshaw buggies, the name I'm using. (Locals call them "*motorcarros*.") They stream like a swarm of insects along the streets. They are the transportation of choice—like no other city I've seen. They are identical for the most part, although variations are not rare. Each one is a motorcycle but with twin rear wheels, a seat for 2 (or 3 maybe) behind the motorcycle rider/driver. It's topped with a surrey top, and side curtains to snuggle in the passengers if weather requires it, but very much an "open" vehicle. As they swarm along the street, the tops-on-parade makes you think of a sea of beach umbrellas that has taken to street-swarming. They are quiet, efficient, and ubiquitous. Turn on a dime, park it seems anywhere, any way. The appearance also is like a small buggy. As transportation it's a buggy-top rickshaw operated by a driver on a motorcycle. They make their own lanes of travel and weaving although the traffic is orderly. Cars and buses exist on the streets as relics of big-size machines. The streets belong to the rickshaw buggies.

The town (60,000) is poverty-blighted. One-story buildings connected in a continuous row for the most part (as was common in Lima), ugly, in disrepair, often open-fronted, small dismal shanty-town quality. (I'm sure there are "better neighborhoods.") Some color variations. Often there are small community-like sections of look-alike shanty houses, often with thatched roofs. A clean, well-lighted place it is not; poorly constructed and maintained streets—but at least not filled with garbage piles. The stores are replete with mannequins sporting clothes for sale—sometimes in grid lines, mannequin people dressed to say look at how spiffy I look, or a string of bikini-clad females—or sometimes only the bottom half in ribbon-like attire. It seems obligatory that each store show off its ranking by mannequin-scoring (I've got more mannequins than Joe next door). And they are replicas of blond tall Caucasians—white—and not at all like the surrounding population.

The people in this river town are short, dark and stocky with plenty of variation around that theme. Beautiful skin, large dark eyes with a special whiteness shining around the black pupils. Gleaming white teeth. With pleasant, friendly faces they have a kind and earthy demeanor feeling.

But the numbers! They seem to be pouring out of cornucopia buildings made of sticks and poles and thatched or corrugated rusty tin and concrete honeycomb pockets of box-spaces from which they are manufactured. Unemployment is very high and there seems to be an air of acceptance of this state of things, as though somehow they are doomed to have, and to meet, low expectations. Often one is approached by little boys in your face pleading with you to buy a T-shirt or a map or what-have-you (or have-not-and-don't-want). Occasionally someone resorts to outright begging.

The bus begins its drive away from town heading to Nauta, 60 miles away, with a stop in the outskirts of Iquitos at an Indian market. The bus has a long bench seat on each side except in the back where there are 2 sets of 2 seats each with a normal forward facing configuration, and, the back row, a single-bench back row somewhat elevated (where I choose to sit, giving me a wide view through both sides and the front). You want to talk about seat-belts, safety requirements, etc? Forget it. The air conditioning is so woeful that finally the windows begin to come open, which in fact produces a pleasant breezy condition (air condition).

The Indian market consists of open stalls of small-room size, dirt floors, thatched roofs—each with its theme of bric-a-brac, jewelry, flutes, bird and animal artifacts, parrots (statuesque, made of various materials) perched in circular loops, some bowls and vases beautifully shining from carved polished wood, etc. You can imagine. Shop owners/clerks seem to be family members, with children a part of the scene. We tourists walk from booth to booth, arousing them to focus, and show and sell. We are not big buyers; I opted to leave empty-handed. The walk-ways are make-shift, with a tree stump or fallen tree or whatever resting here and there. Kind of gloomy. But we are tourists and have our duty to look like shoppers and gawkers.

The trip to Nauta is long and slow. The bus is old but toils away. The road is a two-lane macadam black-top with some traffic, but not heavy. The rickshaw buggies continue to predominate, even outside of town. 30-35 miles per hour is the pace, especially when coming up behind a rickshaw buggy which is often enough. The scenes are especially interesting (2 hours). The land is green, with a busy jumble of hills and ravines, as though an earthquake had moved across the land and gave it a thorough shaking. Thatch-roof open houses on stilts dot the land along the road, although there are long stretches of just countryside. Roadside walkers appear with what seems like a long walking journey—in one case a young woman carrying a small baby, solitary down a long way to go. Many houses seem totally unused. Some houses have a number of people plainly visible from the outside, as though a large family is engaged in just sitting around doing nothing.

The bus rocks and bumps and shakes its way along this simple road that (I heard from the guide) took 60 years to build (60 miles in 60 years), reaching into this not-very-accessible Amazon region.

Occasionally a cow or two is grazing. One scene held 10-15 cows and 2 horses. But mostly there was no sign of agriculture or industry or anything except ghost houses that sometimes contain people, and children without shirts, who look stare-ingly at the bus as it glides by. (Later information suggests that this area is flooded in April-May as the Amazon rises several feet, so this is a factor when seeing houses on stilts and an absence of agriculture, etc.)

Among the things in my backpack is a notebook with writing pad and a sheath of poems that I brought along for some purpose. Maybe this is a purpose moment. So while riding in this old bus in this old land, far far from my customary madding crowd, I wonder what my poems would feel like. A different light, indeed. So I thumb through and read bits and pieces. Is this insightful I'm wondering? What is this poem saying? What is a poem? And why? I think the experience will be some kind of take-away.

At about 130p we reach the little patch-work river-side town-cluster of Nauta, our bus crawling ever so slowly along a very bumpy dirt road to a make-shift-looking dock-place where we board 2 skiffs and cast off to go to our riverboat, *La Turmalina*. It is smaller than I had mental-pictured, 3 decks, green and brown, pretty. A Mississippi gambling boat without a paddlewheel would be its other life.

We're now on the river (which river?—stay tuned). The skiffs-ride to *La Turmalina* gives us a sense of having come to the Amazon. The "moment." A wide reach of river-water creating a sense of sprawling and continuing—a place where water and wetness reign supreme. It exudes peacefulness, a quietness, an openness. And in the mind is a knowing that this is where the Amazon gathers itself within a vast region of water-forces to grow and flow and become long and big and the creator of a unique experience for life on this planet.

We go to our assigned cabins (selected from a diagram at the time of signing up), proceed promptly to have an emergency safety drill with life jackets, and then go to lunch (2p). The dining room on the 2nd deck stern (near my cabin) is attractive—about 7 tables seating 4 each, and buffet counter for serving the food.

The boat/ship is a toy-like pleasure. The top (3rd) deck is open air—chairs, tables, lounge chairs with a pleasant bar. The 3rd-deck room at the stern behind the bar is the small lecture room, sporting power-point capabilities and chairs. The ship's library (the literature said there is a library) is in this small room and consists of 2 small 2-feet long (3-shelves) bookcases, less than half stocked (with mostly paperback you-never-heard-of-this-one books), at about knee level if you want to bend over.

After lunch we board and cast off in our 2 motor-propelled skiffs to explore the wildlife along the river's edge, while *La Turmalina* quietly floats its stately self at our pace along the upstream.

A few words now about who we are. 16 adults plus Gary who is out guide throughout, plus Brian (evolutionary biologist), his Dominican Republic wife, 16-year-old daughter, 12-year old son, plus 2 indigenous naturalist and one on-board indigenous assistant. From California (LA and SF), Chicago, Wyoming, Connecticut, Maine, Houston (me), all "customers" in the senior citizens range (except one just-graduated-from-Harvard granddaughter who's come to accompany her grandparents). Brian is an evolutionary biologist on the Harvard faculty (occupies the chair vacated by the famous biologist E.O. Wilson who recently retired). Brian is very able, nice, excellent communicator, gives power-point lectures each evening before drinks and music on the 3rd deck—then dinner. His wife and children are good additions. The naturalists are energetic, knowledgeable, likable. Our group consists mostly of Harvard graduates but a few from the National Trust of America organization. Doctors, lawyers, real estate, letter-press artist, amateur painter, amateur poet and sculptor, etc. The question makes its rounds: Why did you come to the Amazon? A significant range of stories of travels—Antarctica, India, South America, Europe, the world. Birding is a prevalent theme.

The biologist family is bi-lingual but the rest of us tourists are (seems to me) English-bound (not counting guides, naturalists). The naturalist guides speak a third language. Their English is thick with their Spanish vowels and intonations—it is certainly not English or Spanish—like the bridge language in music for theme transitions. Truly a third language unto itself. (I'll call it Spanglish, for a lack of originality.) Lively to hear and a struggle to understand at times (especially in my case of hearing difficulties). Not only the flow of Spanishsized-pronunciations but the ceaseless apparent effort of "how-do-you-say" mapping of articulations—work-arounds, re-phrasings, facial signals to ask if per chance you have understood that they are trying to communicate to you. (There is a fourth language I have never heard, it goes without saying, which Spanish-speaking people hear when English-speakers show off their Berlitz training.)

We return to *La Turmalina* for 3rd deck sitting and soaking, pisco sours, Peruvian music by a 3-piece ensemble, a power-point talk/presentation by Professor Farrell[5] in the room aft of the bar, then our first on-board dinner, then cabin and sleep after a very long day, a day chucked full of transition and enjoyment, from Iquitos to our river board home upon a very big river.

Monday, February 22

Writing this now in the pre-breakfast hour in the stillness of the open upper (3rd) deck (covered but open sides with rails). Silently the mass of water is on the move, like a continuous mode of migratory instinct, water with the awakening that its time is here to make its long journey to the Atlantic 2,000 miles across a continent. I keep thinking the word "silence." Numerous small bits of detritus dot the expansive flowing stillness, a veritable lake on the move. The washing, curling, twisting and twirling of water surface-play is a mesmerizing vision of a quick/slow motion show of patterns. The sky overhead hangs out puffs and banks of light and dark clouds with no clear intention. Throughout the whole world everything has taken a time out, while water-on-the-move and sky-as-cloud-playground paste a holistic experience for a man on a boat in the Amazon Basin in early morning.

We board skiffs for a second excursion at 4p for shore excursions. For boarding, there are openings on both sides at mid-ship, first deck, and it's a random balancing of passengers, and each skiff gets a naturalist and skiff motorman. The mix in each skiff gets some random re-shuffling over time, but runs with about 8 or so in each skiff. There is plenty of room, ample for about 20 persons. The skiff is a long flat-bottom aluminum (but wood in appearance) boat with seating on the sides. Twin quietly-humming outboard motors with their brand names—one skiff has Johnson (so, two motors make Johnson & Johnson) and the other has Suzuki. The skiff is extremely maneuverable, like a frisky puppy on a watertop. It can purr along a water-splitting path with rocket-like efficiency. It can stop in a quick whoa. Standing up and walking is not precarious if the boat is slow-moving or stopped. Huckleberry Finn and Jim never had it this good.

The excursion is scheduled for 1½ hours, peering and scanning the thick foliage of the river bank, searching for bird-sightings and perhaps other animals, the naturalist moving about the boat, exclaiming and pointing look look look, helping each one of us as needed to train our eyes along the vision-points of big trees, large branches, bushy tops, "3-o'clock" type directions, spots for binocular searching. Then, another exclamation. A black-collared hawk. See, there in that tree (pointing excitedly), just above the big branch about half way up. More and more. Stop it! We can't feast that fast.

So here it goes.

White-wing swallow, white-wing parakeets, Amazon turkey Vulture, yellow-breasted tern, brown-breasted something, half-clad brown father with 3 naked children taking a bath in the same-color river,

Amazon pigmy squirrel, paper wasp nest, passion flower, capped heron, brown-throated 3-toed sloth—many more as sightings and names fly about the binoculars straining about the leaves, branches, banks. I don't see it. Yes, I see it. Now look over there at that . . . .

and the skiff slides its grace along the old water, humming softly the Amazon wildlife tune. A sense that this is the headwaters of life's womb where being is batted about like so much confetti pouring into that stream of miracles. And this is just a warm-up excursion.

Back to *La Turmalina*, pisco sour time followed by lecture. Brian's power-point photos and overview information further whet the wonder of this hyper-active spawning spot.[6] We are present in one of the several rain forest preserves/parks in gigantic numbers of hectors and other dimensions in this region. Information about national and international efforts to preserve and even rescue this unique, huge, lush and wondrous place on earth, which seems destined, perhaps, to be a story that our descendants will only hear about. But Brian is optimistic, full of information about international tax-credits and other measures that hopefully will ride in to the rescue before it's too late. Then dinner, pleasant visit with dinner companions. After dinner the Spanklish talk of next-day activities and questing. (What did he say, I ask my dinner companion? Oh well, you don't know either.) And then to the retiring room where I spend some pre-sleep time doing what you're reading.

Tuesday, February 23

Now I'm sitting on the 3rd deck floating (steaming?) up the river in the afternoon. 2 skiffs have just departed, leaving me alone (it seems, and I may be, except for some crew down below). This departing excursion is Piranha fishing with a gang of enthusiasts. Flesh-eating pack of humans. Gary said to me (as he was confirming my decision to remain behind) we'll catch some Piranha for our dinner. I said, that's why I can't go. If I participate in the capture and killing, I can't then go home and eat them. It's an annoying part of my culinary idiosyncrasies, sometimes ruling out meat and fish altogether (even though I'm not personally involved in the acts), depending, it seems on the phases of the moon or some such non-explanation.

Now *La Turmalina* is parked (tied up) by sticking the bowsprit (a dragon-like neck and head that gives *La Turmalina* a Viking spirit of onward) into a slight inlet with one of my deck-sides brushing against the jungle growth. The engine is powered down and we are at rest, waiting for the fishermen to return. I am looking out upon an Amazonian river that even dominates in scale all of that jungle through which it runs, a fabric of quietude with nits of bird sounds, wafting under a spangle of low hanging clouds. I will remember this place and moment.

The fishermen returned empty-handed. Piranhas were not biting (probably more correct to say, Piranhas were not there, because Piranhas bite when they are there, as I understand it). After a bit, a 6p Brian lecture began. It was a mind expanding input. The topic is how sound in the natural world populates the spectra of decibels and hertz. He had spectrograms on power-point with speakers that matched. Much information about ranges, species (including humans) and the roles of auditory communications. There is another world out there. Insects have a busy cacophony. All animals communicate, and are busy doing so. They have to compete for spots and time on the bandwidths, and have methods to work around when the airways are too crowded, which is often, or even usual. We are relatively new at the game of understanding all of this, but it's opening important windows to biodiversity and evolution (Brian's focus).

Afterwards, a second evening of Peruvian music. Singers (male), guitar, banjo, flute and moroccas (don't know the word although I should and may try to look this up: it's the hand-held object that rattles along with the music beat when shaken, often a part of South American music). It is lively and pleasant, and the flute is a delightful presence. A nice setting, under the black night, covered by a riverboat's roof with whirling ceiling fans, a breeze, and the awareness of enjoying Peruvian music at night on a river boat in Amazonia.

Then dinner. Then the skiffs take us for a night ride, using lights to see the river banks. After some futility, we (someone with amazing ability) spot a snake in a tree, so we look for a while. Then we (that remarkable someone) spot a frog, bring it on board, and another (different type). I have pictures. A silent full moon barely showing itself through the clouds. And one star, which no one points to.

Wednesday, February 24

Now I'm on the 3rd deck again with a beer (Iquitena—there is a choice of only this one, so with effort I made my decision), pre-lunch, where the breeze is soft and the scene is placid. (Who invented frenetic?)

    This morning we had an excursion along the bird-sighting river bank, dis-embarking to enter a butterfly garden (enclosed by netting) and microcosm focus on the abundance that resides within. Brian is the star. (At dinner last night he came 3 times to my table showing each time a specimen he had taken from the ship's rail or somewhere outside the dining room. Part of the message was: this kind of stuff is all about us. It is delightful, as Brian shares his knowledge and wonder with show-and-tell of tiny creatures.) In the butterfly garden he could, and did, make us aware of the zone of life intensities playing out beneath our range of normal radar. As we are about to depart the netted tent, Eric (one of the local naturalists) had us hold hands, prayer-like, for a ceremony (repeat after me) to recite a wish for the life and prosperity of butterflies. As allowed, the 12 or so translucent plastic containers (roughly quart size) were handed to us (the ones used in the talk about the butterfly garden when we entered), and the point was to step outside, lift the lid, and watch the butterfly rise away to wherever it is that butterflies wish to go when they can go where they wish.

    Now, just now, the rain has come, the first since our arrival. Soft re-assuring rain stretching across the broad broad river above which the clouds and light hold their breath. In the distance a small murmuring motor canoe slowly drawing a line in the water as it makes its solitary journey across the scene.

From the butterfly garden we walk along a long wooden bridge with side-rails over a water-bottom jungle. A few spider monkeys make a curiosity out of us, on the bridge and in the trees, keeping a little out of our way. This leads to a sloping stretch down to the edge of a lake. We mount canoes (joined together 2 canoes each, to made a stability) and in a flotilla of 3 such, we paddle (a young man—boy?—at the stern is the principal paddler) into the environs. Lots of sightings. Turtles, fish jumping often about the lake, Giant Guinea Pig (or is it a giant rodent, or is this the same?). And then on the other side, in a dense grove, we see a colony of these animals keeping an eye on us. Lots of sightings of birds and birds. About an hour of this; then we go back ashore, trek a short distance and board skiffs for the return home, dawdling along the river's edge for sightings. One fairly spectacular sighting of a tree full of beautiful parrot-size feather-crested bird whose name for some reason is only given in Spanish, beyond my grasp.

The mid-day break with lunch. This is where I'll choose to talk about the rivers. The Amazon is fed and created, as we would surmise even if we were not seeing it before our eyes, by other large rivers. The 2 principal ones are Rio Marañón and Rio Ucayali, and their convergence IS THE BEGINNING OF THE AMAZON. The town (Nauta), to which we arrived by bus from Iquitos, is on the Marañón. This has been our river so far. It is itself quite near the Amazon, and the Amazon flows eastward, passing near Iquitos some 50 miles or so downstream.) I have yet to learn if my trip to the Amazon will take me to the Amazon. A brief discussion with Brian's wife as we boarded our skiffs in Nauta was something to the effect that it's all Amazon here—it's the Amazon Basin, the cradle of Amazonia. I begin to see that that is so.

THURSDAY, FEBRUARY 25

Up at 6. Had decided to miss the birding excursion (6-8), so I had the morning alone on the upper deck, which I've come to enjoy a lot. Breakfast at 8 (as birders return and join in). Between 9 and 10, a talk by Eric (native naturalist/leader) to provide general history, culture on ecological overview to focus in due course on village life, people and activity, to prepare for the short skiff ride to a village from 10-1230.

There is a lot to say about this village experience. 20 of us (say) motoring to a 12-15 feet high river bank where several small children begin to gather, each side gawking at the other side. We the gringos with hats, sunglasses, cameras, binoculars, water bottles, tourist attire in sneakers and hiking boots. Our guide is very good at interacting and interpreting. An elderly dumpy woman, clad in old seemingly dirty clothes, snaggle-toothed, 62 years old, 11 children, was the main contact. We walk with talk close by to see and learn about 2-dug-out canoes, the machete, how it's kept sharp, and various fruit-bearing trees. There is a very small orchard-like stand of Yucca trees (10-12 feet high), and the old woman with her machete demonstrates cutting one (the cut-off stalk, 2"or so thick), then she pulls the 1" stump/stalk, raising its roots out of the soft moist loam, exposing the roots which are the highly valued food (like potatoes are harvested). She demonstrates peeling (quick slicing with the machete), and our guide talks about the Yucca's many uses, including a 5% alcoholic "beer" (fermented with spittle). She uses the upper cut-off part to plant (easily) a new tree, which takes about 6 months to grow to maturity.

Walking on, children moving with us, intermingling, to her house on stilts. She invites us (all of us) up the wooden stairs (6 feet elevation) into her living room. The house is stout, well-built, consisting of 4 rooms. The predominantly large living room is about 10 x 20, has bags of rice in one section, various items here and there on the floor—no furniture. Wooden boards as floor, open sides (waist high to ceiling). Actually there is no ceiling except the underside of a steep-peaked thatched roof, with a attic-like openness above the living room and 2 contiguous smaller rooms (bedrooms, mainly, but also various things are stored). Construction is poles wrapped together at joints, most of them are strong 4" diameter long poles, a special wood, we're told. A wooden bamboo-like partitioning of rooms. The kitchen is sort of separate (as though an add-on), a duck-your-head walk across a short gang-plank-like connection to a platform, about 10 x 10—completely open for about half of the platform like a porch. A central raised hearth, 3 or 4 feet high, rectangular, is for cooking, with ashes on which sit a kettle and a pot. Partially used stalk of small bananas on the floor nearby, as well as, further away, a small amount of lemons, or lemon-like fruit. Various "junk" items lie around. The kitchen has a separate thatched peak roof. The house seems to serve as living quarters, storehouse, and way-station, all in one. Clothes are hanging over the living room wall/rail on one end for drying (washed where? In the river probably? River water at least.). Thatching is from palm-tree leaves. A roof lasts about 6 years if the roof is steeply peaked. Thatching consistently has a well-constructed, tight, workmanlike quality.

I'll splice in here a conversation I had with Eric (our native guide/leader, about 35 years old) at breakfast. I sat alone, having entered in advance of the returning birders, so he very politely joined me. We chatted about this and that. I asked him to tell me about the necklace on his neck. A leather loop holding a 2" tooth. He says it is a Caiman tooth which he wears for protection, and luck, long life. With careful and sensitive phrasing I ask him, do you believe in that? He gets the point and is willing, even eager, to respond. 50-50 he says. It actually relates to the environment in which he lives, the oneness that he feels and his desire to feel. The Caiman tooth (a long one because the longer the tooth, the longer his life) is symbolic of the patience that a Caiman has. He sits motionlessly and waits. Eric wants to emulate this. He makes references to elaborate on this point to spiders and their webs, to anacondas who secrete themselves into a shollow pool of water to wait for the moment when an animal appears to take a drink, and then it strikes, after the obligatory exercise of long patience. So the Caiman (and some other species) must know and practice patience and then, when the moment comes, go to it, take your prize. He contrasts this to predators that pursue, that pro-actively seek their prey. Eric emulates—wants to emulate the patient type—watch, lying in wait—and the Caiman tooth emblem around his neck empowers his commitment to living this way. And comfort by knowing that the karma that it imparts to him is good. And that he is woven into the fabric of nature itself.

So what are your thoughts? Different kinds of people? Or, a characteristic of Amazonian way of thinking? We are now going to resume our visit of this small Amazonian village, having in mind, who are these people?

(I'm aware, of course, that this observation is only a singularity start of a much larger picture, but it comes to me and provides to me a tone or theme for thinking about this place.)

In the old woman's house we heard about daily life, building and maintenance. There are some 30 families, about 200 people. Today we see only 5-10 adult women, 15-20 children 12 and under generally. A wide walking grass space (street?) with 6-8 houses, 2 having poles in the ground with some connections beginning, that indicate new construction. The men (teenage boys as well it seems) are absent, presumably at their respective jobs or elsewhere schools (daily commute?). Some neighboring houses are replete with scroungy, ugly chickens, a few short-haired dogs (16" or so). One house has a small pigpen, in addition to wandering chickens and lying-around dogs, as part of the under-the-house barnyard. I had to stand off to avoid the chicken/pig stench. However, notwithstanding this instant case, generally the area is clean, green and pretty. The houses are minimalist but attractive and inviting, a sense of relaxed spaciousness. (A romantic South Sea feel?) We walked to the soccer field. (Eric, in his talking to us, asks, if we know the 2nd religion of Peru—Catholicism comprising 90%? Answer: soccer.) The school house, located on the far edge of the closely-clipped grass soccer field, is not a pole-supported thatched roof structure. It's a pre-fab (seems) low-roof one-room (but very long—40-50 feet) blue colored neat structure with lots of windows.

Our guide, Eric, assembles the available children (10 girls, 8 boys, say) in gender lines by size-ranking, facing our 20-person cruise-ship entourage for interaction. With help from them, we learn how to count to 10 in Spanish (surpisingly, there is little Spanish-speaking in our group), and one of us is selected by a child for a pop quiz. Then one of us leads the teaching to the children of counting to 10 in English. Then we sing to each other. Our group selects and sings "You Are My Sunshine." They did a Spanish version of: If you want to . . . , clap your hands, etc" tune. (Sorry. At the moment my memory is hiding a few words.) Instead of "Clap your hands" they sing *Esta bien* for which we are invited to provide the choral part. Then Eric does bio sketching (name, age, grade) child by child, translating in summary each child's response. Then attention goes to a table under a large magnificent stand-alone tree at the edge of the soccer field, where local hand-made artifacts (necklaces and bracelets, mostly) are offered for sale by the children. With Edie Jane in mind I step right up and engage in a financial transaction with a very pretty 9-year-old smiling, black-haired, white teeth, black/brown eyes-surrounded-by-snow female child as precious as anything on earth. 10 sols each. The Peruvian word for their currency and its English sound-alike word does not escape me.

So who are these people? The demographics speak of concentrations of populations in Lima and other urban points. The per capita population for each square mile in the Amazon region is miniscule. 2 of the boys who were introduced travel the water by dug-out canoe to a "distant" school. Eric constantly remarks on the friendliness, openness, welcomingness, supportiveness, etc., of the people. The village-viewing certainly supports his characterizations. I also think thoughts of the breakfast talk with Eric—patience—waiting for life to drift something your way. Fruit and soil and water and poles and palm leaves are lying about the landscape, just to be picked up, in a smooth and non-threatening climate. Canoes and plentiful fish for spearing. Nowhere to go, no need to go. Easy life, small needs, you can do all you need to do, and have all you need to have, just by waiting patiently.

As our skiff moves away from the bank, I wonder if I hear a child ask her mother: *Quien son esas personas?*

(I am writing this on the 3rd deck, 3p, a glass of *ceveza* at my side, ship beginning to move, the transitioning experience—more like the jungle and river landscape scene beginning to glide across my vision—smooth and serene AND I have donned my Bose headphones and ipod, listening to operatic arias as I float "upstream" along the Amazon. I'm taking a break to gaze and gaze.)

At 4p we launch our overnight-in-the-rainforest excursion. Skiffs take us to a bank, then canoes take us across a small lake, and we begin a trek of about 1 and ½ hours to the camp site. The walk as usual frequently stops because someone (usually a naturalist, but others too) spot a spider or a bird or a tree or a something worthy of comment and a little discussion. Very typical of our many walks in the jungle. At nightfall (6p, but in the rainforest the light goes away early because of the thickness overhead) we reach the camp—multiple "tents" (as they are called but in fact they are small cubicle huts with thatched roofs and layers of mosquito netting etc, with a dual zipper entrance way). Each hut (tent) is connected by a short wooden gangplank to an outside bathroom. Inside my tent are 2 bunk-beds with gleaming white sheets etc, and a made-in-China battery-powered miniature lantern. Press the top, you have light; press the top, it goes off. I was loaned a flashlight to traverse the paths after dark (not bringing one along which, so far, has been my only sin of packing omission). (Paths usually consist of round slices of tree-trunks as stepping stones, some solid, some decaying, some sunk.) After "checking in" (i.e., depositing my backpack) I go to the main building 20 feet away—a screened in structure about 20 x 35 with tables and at one end a rather complete kitchen, including a 6 x 6 area for cooking using open wood-burning.

Dinner consists of a special local dish made of rice, chicken and other ingredients, compacted into a ball by 2 large leafs that hold it for cooking, and impart to the dish a flavor. (Sorry I do not grasp the names or the recipe.) The chef makes a demonstration (cooking lesson) of the process, using 2 of our group to participate (help). This dish, plus plantains (coated with crystallized brown sugar) and vegetables comprise a pleasant dinner in a low-light convivial room. I had a bottle of Merlot in the shipboard reserve which they brought for my pleasure (and Peter's, sitting across from me.)

After dinner a 1-hour walk in the night rainforest. How they manage to spot anything is amazing (each of us has a flashlight) but they do—frogs, spiders and their webs. Mostly the focus is on night sounds of the rainforest, and the talk of related information. Who hunts at night, and why and how. The communications embedded in the sounds. There is a lot of animal life filling up the airwaves, especially if you listen.

Early to bed and early to rise. Pitch black nighttime. To bed at 830, awake at 5. At 512, a rain in the rainforest begins, at times a very hard rain. I lie on my bed soaking in the sound and place-awareness. Rain, rainforest, dark, a fine low nuzzling tune of life's abundant presence surrounding me.

We had planned a pre-breakfast walk, with a 530 wake-up call. But the rain changes that. (I think the rain is a welcome reason to sleep in.) I go to the main room for coffee at 6, with an opportunity for a quiet visit with Victor, one of our naturalists, and awareness of the rain. Breakfast being prepared over the open in-door fireplace. People begin drifting in by about 7 or so, rain stops, good breakfast, then departure for our morning trek through the jungle.

Skiffs and canoes, bird sightings. The lake water we canoe across is mirrow-still, and black, but, like black can do, light bounces clearly off its surface. A couple of my photos show a water reflection of the shore and sky that almost outdoes the actual shore and sky.

The main feature of this extended walk is the traversing of a series of suspension foot bridges, one after another, viewing the rainforest down below from our scenic highway. Orchids, trees, water, sounds, birds, a sense of being so lucky to be able to absorb a top-of-the-Amazon-rainforest morning in the company of good naturalists.

Arriving at 1130 to a compound with a large main building in the jungle. Never quite figure out what it does—maybe it's an Amazon hotel/lodge. Here we have a shaman presentation/ceremony (while we sit in a three/quarter circle), described below. A display of handmade artifacts for sale (I bought one). Lunch (including a large "whole" baked Piranha, vegetables, etc. I decided to harden my heart and eat some of it (partly because, if the roles were reversed, it would eat some of me). (I won't bother to note that this Piranha is the fruit-eating variety; it would spoil my excuse.)

Lunch is a very pleasant open-air cone-ceiling attractive building. (I can't linger on its unusual and well-designed, well-constructed features.) Peruvian music by a 3-piece (typical) band, pisco sours, wine and after-dinner Bailey's. Not bad for a rainforest morning. After lunch Victor and the band inveigle some of our group to dance to the Latin rhythms of the Peruvian band. A party is going on.

All good things come to an end, or, in this case, a transition. We get the leader's signals, gather our backpacks and march to the lake for the canoe-then-skiffs return to La Turmalina. 2p.

I'll backtrack. The shaman is 55 years old, dressed in a grass skirt and no shirt. Bare feet. Very very simple. He has an assistant, an Indian woman about the same age, maybe 10 years younger. Again, simple attire. Rosario (our Spanglish-speaking sometimes announcer, organizer) acts as MC. Shaman spoke to us, softly, slowly, with liquid hand and arm movements. Rosario tries but is not quite successful in translating. His language is from his native area in northern Peru, near Ecuador. He has lived in this area about 15 years. His language is one of a multitude of Amazonian and Peruvian languages/dialects, that are gradually giving way to Peru's *linqua franca*—Spanish. He then repeats his remarks in Spanish, although it is said that his Spanish is minimal. Rosario translates this, of course, telling of his years of training (asceticism, isolated and simple living, etc). His assistant speaks a different Indian language and no Spanish, so they are unable to communicate verbally with one another except spottily.

Shaman's ceremony then begins. He and his assistant kneel in a prayer position, communing personally with spirits (although no talk of deities or other-worldliness). A jar of dark liquid is exhibited with descriptions of its arcane and indigenous ingredients, able to transport one into an hallucinatory state and visions. This drink is for shaman-consumption only—patients don't imbibe. (There is talk about healing capabilities, herbal medicines, etc.) It is passed around so we can smell. Shaman then uses a small clutch of leaves in his hand to shake over the head/face of each of us, one at a time, while chanting, while his assistant walks behind us, and in unison with Shaman's incantations, blows smoke from the special cigarette she lit for the occasion—blowing the smoke into the back of each head. This done, shaman then makes the circle again, one by one, cupping his hands over our (in each case) cupped hands, pronouncing something (having to do with, have a good life). The assistant stands in the middle, sing-chanting. When shaman finishes, he joins his assistant for a few bars of duet sing-chanting.

This accomplished, we are all blessed and spirited onward into our lives of bliss.

I would not repress my silent thoughts: incredibly silly! (It's in my mind to wonder about what is reality—the real world—and wonder who will cast the first stone?)

Back to *La Turmalina*, Siesta time (what, with all the drinks?) However, I feel okay and ready to write this.

At this moment I'm on the 3rd deck, having been "floating" upstream. Rio Marañón has become much more narrow, of course. But it is still dominatingly huge. I'm guessing 400-500 yards wide, or more. Strong current. Lots of water.

Next event, a 4p skiff ride if interested, and I decide to enjoy *La Turmalina*.

Then the 6p Brian power-point lecture and Q & A.[7] Topic is biodiversity and building the catalogue. Famous E. O. Wilson of Harvard (Brian succeeded to Wilson's chair) has inaugurated a type of encyclopedia (some Wikipedia aspects, but more rigid filters). Brian begins with a Mars photo that got a lot of press because it has the precious hint of life. Then, how much we spend to send robots to Mars, the budget for humans to go, etc. Compared to: why not visit our own planet? How much we don't know is enormous. Species to be found, identified, catalogued. Numbers are mind-boggling—how much there is (as well as its disappearance rate). Reasons to capture this whole information are plentiful. For instance, in today's flat world, insects travel. (Brian gives an example of a beetle type from China that is invading New England with serious adverse consequences, which created a very pro-active program to try to stem it. How would we know of invasions if we do not know what the indigenous population consists of at any given time-slot?) Brian is amazing in his knowledge and presentation skills. A good Q & A. I'm sitting with a question incubating that won't quite hatch. It has to do with management capabilities of, let's say, an overload of information and its velocity of change (analogous to our effort to mount computer capability for weather forecasting). I applaud Brian's school of thought and enterprise, and would not want to sound negative with a question like: well, if we collect and store all of this humongous data base in its dynamically changing storehouse, how do we sort it, sift it, apply it, make it usable? While this would have a negative sound, the thought is not negative; it intends only to say, what a challenge this is. Of course, we have to do all we can to do what we can and the reasons are compelling, even dire. Again, a very interesting information presentation, of which Brian has many to give.

Then dinner, pleasant visiting, announcements of next day's activities. Highlight: beginning at 630 next morning we have a 4-hour skiffing of upstream tributaries, deeper jungle, and view of early morning river.

What Day? And look back at overnight

630a skiff boarding. About 13 in our skiff when the time comes, including the naturalist (Victor), the operator and 2 young men to shepherd and serve our breakfast. We cast off. Describing the next 4 hours is challenging to me now.

First, an overview. We are proceeding for a short time on the Tigre River (which flows into the Marañón River, which combines with the Ucayali River at the downstream confluence to be the Amazon). We soon leave the main stream (quite wide at this point—guessing ¼ mile or more) and take a tributary—100 yards wide, quickly getting more narrow. I ask Victor: am I wrong? Isn't the water flowing away from the big river "into which it's supposed to flow"? He replies affirmatively, saying the big river's rising water is backing water into the upstream of its tributaries. It's a long course (again, 4 hours round trip) into the back-reaches of the wetlands. Very wet, as in swamp-like, as we journey deeper and deeper. Vegetation is thick, diverse, high reaching, vine-embroiled, water-rooted—teeming and streaming from its source of some hidden powerful (magisterial, mystical) force whose role it is from the other side of the threshold to push unceasingly into this world more and more and more.

Birding. The early morning is a thriving, robust bonanza of avian activity. They fly overhead this way and that way. Toucans, hawks, woodpeckers, and many other names bandied about by our naturalist and 2 or 3 other experienced watchers. The skiff's flat-bottom 5-foot beam allows standing as we cruise slowly, turning about as needed, overhead this side, that side, both sides, overhead. We alter speed when the naturalist silently gives signals to the operator.

The language of species identification, mentioned above, is fascinating and mellifluous, with words that grab the distinctive features—often color—to tag a species with its appellation. The banter of words goes on and on. Victor exclaims op.op.op.op.op..look.look.little guy..little guy, as he's pointing energetically. (Actually, "iddle/g'y..iddleg'y..iddleg'y" in Spanglish.) From the zone of birding ability that I have (or don't have) I can see, enjoy and learn. It's like the frequent sweeping into the skiff of a breeze of shared excitement, pointing, describing, exclaiming, trying to help one another locate the spotted bird. Some are better than others at spotting, and at being able to find the bird that the pointer-outer is pointing to. Moving from naked eye to binoculars is a learning curve. How do you fix the binoculars onto the spot "on the branch to the right just above the green bushy place about 15 feet up" and so forth. My binoculars are very satisfying to me. I gradually improve my skill of going to the objective. I would give me a grade for finding the bird is at times as good as 50-50, which means a lot of misses. I am not alone in this struggle. I am amazed at Victor's skill. I fantasize that at one point I exclaim: look, look—pointing with authority—a yellow-tufted white-wing Amazon Eagle, just there, perched in the bonzo tree, watching the family of Cappuccino Monkeys in the trees below. And everyone ooo's and ahhh's, murmuring what eyesight I have, what skill to locate this extraordinary and rarely sighted creature in the Amazon Rainforest. Waking up, I snap back to trying some more to improve my score at fixing my binoculars on something or other that is being called by a beautiful name from the robust and voluminous glossary of bird watchers.

(I cannot do a yeoman job of accounting for the variety and instances of sightings, so my apology to any reader who craves this information. It would be a rich accounting.)

In addition to birds we have 3 or 4 occasions of monkey-sightings, usually a family or small colony size, much screened by the verdancy and thickness of their arboreal habitat. Victor spotted a large dark knot among other knots dotting the trunk uprise of a very tall light-bark tree about 30 feet high which houses a yellow-crown brush-tail rat, poking its head out of a hole, about two inches in opening. How could Victor spot this as we skiff along the water? At breakfast tie-up, we are in a wider-than-usual expanse of water while pink dolphins move about the area. When one flips out of the water, the sight is quickly gone, consisting of a surface splash of water, a pink something, a quick disappearance. Leaving one to wonder while scanning the black reflective water surface, where will the next moment occur?

Breakfast at 830-9. Each one is served a lap tray. (Remember we sit along the benches attached to the skiff's gunnels which are about 2-3 feet high, 40 feet long, a walking beam platform about 5 feet wide, and a cross-beam at mid-pint to hold a table cloth and assorted condiments.) Coffee, a roll, 2 sandwiches (ham and cheese, chicken), orange juice, a tangerine-like fruit (outside it looks like a lime). If you consider the location it's a mighty fine restaurant. The other skiff ties up nearby and we swap some joculars about how our sightings are far better than their sightings, starting innocently enough, then escalating to nonsense hyperboles (like jaguars, then polar bears).

I need to talk about the sounds. The scene is one of quietness hanging over us but there is also contained within this vastness a flittering of vocal pop-ups and quick-tune calls, the *bel cantos* of this wilderness. Sometimes a tune is bold and prominent, evoking a "what's that"? It's as though we are in a vast open Amazon water-laden rainforest jungle, warped by solitude, wherein beautiful sounding wind instruments, made of wild and wonderful birds, are making a performance for us. Thank you. Thank you.

The after-breakfast presents more as we travel even deeper into the narrowing water-path of the jungle. This kind of penetration may explain the timing—late February—of our Amazon expedition—when water level is about average, so that we can have a penetration. The river is due to rise 10-15 feet higher I've heard it said, reaching its peak in mid-May. I don't know now why mid-May would not be more suitable. I assume the depth of the dry season would not be good because the "low water" access would be limiting. There are factors, and I'm not up to sorting this out. In any case we seem to be at the deep reach of our water-path, sufficiently enwrapped by jungle mania and animal presence.

At 1015a Victor gives the take-us-to-*La Trumalina* signal and the skiff gets revved up. Upon our return-home boarding we have about 30 minutes before the talk that is scheduled for 11—it got moved to 1130. Eric uses large easel-stand maps in the bar area of the 3rd deck to present a "recap." He traces our journey from our arrival to the river on day one through today's morning excursion and on to the end. Flash: *La Turmalina* will sail on the Amazon—later today! Going a ways downstream from the confluence point. The Amazon actually starts 2,000 miles southwardly along the Andes (different names for various stretches of the river winding its way northward into the northeast section of Peru which is the Amazon

Basin (here). The Amazon Basin has a huge presence in Brazil as well, and reaches the border boundaries of Ecuador and Columbia. The Amazon Basin gathers water from both the South and the North—from the North it flows southward from about latitude "0" and from the South it flows northward from about 16 degrees south latitude. When it assumes its formal name at the confluence of Rio Marañón and Rio Ucayali (and I am located right now at this proximity) it starts its 2300-mile journey to the Atlantic.

Lunch next, then announcements of a Piranha fishing trip, 3-550p, for those who want it (and it's popular). The second time to try to bring some home. I am on the 3rd deck (surprised?). *La Turmalina* is tied up to the bank (just now) on the side of a very wide river. During some of our afternoon river cruise a thunderstorm played across the not-too-distant sky—beautiful clouds, lightening and some thunder sounds, having from its perch quite a view of the Amazon Basin.

Lecture by Brian at 620p (running a little late because the fishermen had a good harvest and got home late). Topic is vanishing species.[8] (Piranha species?) Brian has a positive outlook generally and it did not fail him on this topic. He shows graphs and statistics regarding collapsing species of overfished oceans, recovery prospects in the context of the rate of recovery when a moratorium is invoked, the aggregate picture of all fish in the overfished oceans, our experience with learning the critical mass threshold when the population of a species can no longer sustain itself, etc. He cited names and organizations and activities that have risen or are rising to the challenge, programs of foreign debt forgiveness that facilitates retaining or restoring wildlife habitats. He presents maps of NASA photographs to show population distribution around the globe by light distribution at night, and shows that this (i.e., absence of light) coincides with the distribution of the earth's concentrations of wildlife resources in need of protection. One point is explained by "the tragedy of the commons" as follows. The English Lord sets aside a "common" available free to the community for cattle grazing. Since it's free and no one is responsible for consequences, it becomes overgrazed. The absence of stewardship ethics and responsibility results in tragedy—the commons is ruined as a resource.

Dinner and announcements regarding the next day.

Friday, February 26

La Turmalina was tied up overnight at the land between the two rivers that form the Amazon. We take the Ucayali tributary upstream for about 2 hours during breakfast, etc.

This is the last day before departure/travel day. We board the skiffs at 930 for a 2-hour excursion. After a 15-minute travel by skiff we disembark onto a riverbank fortified by jungle. The experience is to walk across a flat land of rainforest floor, and to see a lagoon with giant lily pads—the largest in the world. We have our regular local guides, Victor and Brian, and we meet a local local guide for more up-close contact.

The jungle is real jungle, having a twilight amount of light. A large variety of trees (of course), vines in profusion, flowers, undergrowth—great flora diversity and density. As the water continues to rise during the next 2½ months this area will be about 10-15 feet under water. Obviously it handles this successfully every year. We receive identification and other information regarding items of interest, such as medicinal properties, etc. Bird sounds are prevalent. It's not hard to know we are on the floor of a dense rainforest in the Amazon.

The lily pond, or lagoon, is an area about 30 x 50 yards beyond which is a thick carpet of tall water grass. The lilies are about 3 feet or so in diameter floating close to each other. They are entirely water plants—not connected to the bottom. While enjoying this scene we are entertained by a small group (7 or so) of brightly colored robin-size birds. 2 colors per bird: black and yellow. The colors have such depth and strength that they seem gem-like. The name is yellow-rump tacique. They have highly vocal and active song-making skills. They are "mocking birds" and Victor says they can mimic the sound of up to 50 birds. They seem to be focused on a nearby paper wasp nest for feeding (in some way not clear to me). We observe several minutes of silence—the peace, the beauty, the entertainment by spectacular busy birds, and, I add, an awareness that this particular jungle walk, lily pad and bird visit, is a final Amazon rainforest foray (for us, this trip).

We then trek for about 20 minutes—looking, spotting, learning—to re-board the skiff and return to *La Turmalina*.

Lunch, announcements about the afternoon—packing, 4p recap talk, 6p music entertainment with pisco sours, 7p dinner, and bed. Tomorrow morning, suitcases are to be placed outside the cabin at 715, departure at 830 by bus for the 1½ hour ride to the Iquitos airport to go to Lima, to arrive at Hotel

Sonesta El Olivar at about 5 or so and a group farewell dinner on the coast. There will be 8 of us who are traveling the next day to Cusco to overnight at the hotel. The U. S. bound passengers will go from dinner to the airport for post-midnight departures.

For the recap, Eric placed the big map on the easel stand and numbered as he talked the sequences of our activities—left Iquitos (1), bused to Nauta (2), took the boat up Rio Marañón to point x where he inserted a "3." Last number was 20 as we moved along the mat of thick and thin artery lines that gather water that grows to become the Amazon, as we re-live our activities of bird watching, butterfly foray, walk-ways across the top of rainforest, camp-out in the midst of jungle darkness, skiffing and canoeing along rivers and lakes, visiting a village, witnessing a shaman ceremony, walking the dimly-lit floor of the rainforest, and on and on. I could add many more numbers to place pinpoints on my memory map of this experience. Brian's lectures helped the whole experience—were informative, thought provoking, altering our insights and perspectives of the Amazon, and even beyond.

From the re-cap on the open 3rd deck we convened in the lecture room for one more Brian power-point presentation[9]—reviewing sounds we were exposed to which he had recorded, displaying concomitantly the visual and sound spectra where lines and blips appear in characterizing array. For example, during our night-stay in the jungle and related walk, the sounds of bats occurring at night are not audible to humans, but their appearances could be noted by the blips located high on the graph marking their entering and leaving the night scene, unnoticed by us at the time. Low tone frog sounds occupy thick splotches of spectra studded along the base (base?). The spectrograph trains along a time line slowly, with rich color, informing us that there is a world of sound that is playing out that we are hardly conscious of and, indeed, that to some extent it exists outside of our auditory perception boundaries. It's fascinating to become significantly more aware of the acoustical depth and range of the life that surrounds us, and the working out of vocal strategies in the rich diversity.

Brian then played for us a short selection of sound tracks that can be obtained commercially for Itune use: birds and whales.

After Brian, we returned to the outside deck for Pisco sours and Peruvian music. Then dinner and announcements about the departure next morning.

Day of departure, saying goodbye to *La Turmalina*, our home on the river that has been good to us. Saying goodbye to the Amazon. It, too, has been good to us.

Now we board the old bus to go 60 miles to the Iquitos airport, and hope that it will be good to us.

The last-minute act before departing is to gather on the stairway that leads up from the 2ⁿᵈ deck to the 3ʳᵈ deck, where we are facing the bowsprit, for our family photo.

I am writing now, not on the 3ʳᵈ deck, but in the airport of Iquitos at 11a after a bus trip through lush countryside, the same as we traveled when going from Iquitos to Nauta.

(I have to insert that I pulled from my back pack on the bus a sheath of poems [poems-in-progress] thinking [as I did on the journey to Nauta] that the feel of how some of them read in this big-shift [for me] environment might be insightful. It happens that I dwell on the first one ["Nothing Pines for Something"—current title]. By the end of the trip, I had made several good [I think] revisions. This was interesting to me. I have looked at this poem numerous times, for the most part continuing to think of it as it is. This time something went to work that sharpened my sense of intention and language clean-up—a heightened grasp of the poem's role. Leaves me wondering [for the millionenth time] about how to open my mind to see what's already dwelling therein? I wish I could be moved into this mode more often. Does it require a trip to the Amazon?)

The small Iquitos airport is privately owned, in its advanced construction phase. Really quite well done—design, material, simplicity, quality—as though catching a moment of "we can do this." A long wait for departure (1245). The snack bar features an array of chips, nuts, ice cream, beer, etc. with tables and chairs in a street-side café style in the well lighted lobby. The locals (lots of children) move about, clean, well turned out, attractive. If this were the only Iquitos I had seen I would have missed the Iquitos that is—an old half-shanty-town, half striving-to-prosper-town on the Amazon, with a long history involving growth, get-rich-quick, boom-bust, natives-migrating-to-city, the-poor-are-always-with-us city. I became aware when traveling the rivers that, from the confluence, the Amazon travels by Iquitos, about a hundred miles downstream from Nauta and the confluence point. At one time Iquitos was an Amazon river-bank city but the Amazon has its ways of changing its pathways and it made a move a short distance from the city. Iquitos has another river (name?) by its side, so all is not lost.

Not much to do but sit and wait, sit and observe, sit and visit, sit and read, sit and write. Announcement that the plane will not arrive until 120. But we are now in the mode of a bunch of sheep tourist, come what may.

Arrive Lima. This time in daylight. Transfer by bus through the busy streets of Lima to Sonesta El Olivar and my assigned room. Now I realize the room I had on my first arrival was a luxury suite (gratis upgrade) and now my room is the standard model, and quite pleasant.

On the bus the local guide information about the 8.8 earthquake in Chile—in the south of, but including, Santiago. Memoires flash back of my 3 days in Santiago in '04 as the gathering point for my trip to Antarctica. The tsunami threat to Hawaii and then Japan is a factor. I get to English CNN in my room. The largest magnitude since 1900 they're saying. Much bigger than the recent one in Haiti. But the area south of Santiago is not densely populated (like Santiago, or Haiti). Death count at the moment is 250-300. The tsunami is now reaching Maui (coastal area has been evacuated) but is only 3 feet high at this moment. Stay tuned. Japan is engaged in big preparation. To cut to the end, it turns out the tsunami did not get significantly worse in Hawaii which, along with Japan, canceled the emergency call. I get the feeling that CNN is saying "Aw, shucks!"

On the bus ride from the airport to El Olivar, a few of our expert birders indeed spotted a multi-colored plentius pigeon, a rare bird perhaps somewhere. Amazing.

Dinner at 7 at a nice restaurant at the coast, jutting out a little over the white wave dancing, looking back on the arteries of lights at the coast-base of a steep high "mountain" side, with plenty of dots of light spread across the mountainside. Some brown pelicans visiting outside our window. Pisco sour, ceviche as appetizer, wine, fish, dessert—too much—I quit after the ceviche, which is quite good. From the parking lot, a few departed for the airport, the rest of us go to El Olivar. The beginnings of goodbyes to freshly bonded friendships. A list with email addresses had been distributed at dinner. Ruminations about chance meetings, transitory friendsips, never-ever-to-meet-again people on earth saying goodbye. The anonymous-author poem comes to mind:

You to the left and I to the right,
for the ways of men must sever.
It well may be for a day and a night,
and it well may be forever.

Sunday, February 28

Wake up call at 530, pack, bag placed outside room down to breakfast, back to room briefly, then gather in lobby for 715 bus loading. 8 of us now, including Gary, our leader—capable, smooth, helpful.

The Lima airport is all that a modern airport can be. It's quite congested, especially for a Sunday morning. The Santiago airport closed due to the earthquake, disrupting and diverting a lot of air traffic, which has a prominent effect on the Lima airport (as is obvious now to us). We learn that 3 of our group who were scheduled to depart at 1230 or so that morning for Las Angeles got re-scheduled to 10a this morning. (Their flight would have originated in Santiago, but a plane was sent from L.A.) Our negotiation through the airport to our on-schedule 940 departure was smooth. The Peruvian crowd is polite and friendly—amiable people.

I'm now at the airport planning to fly from 200 feet above sea level to 11,000 feet above sea level (straight up?). Some talk about high altitude behavior. I had a cup of coca tea at the airport Starbucks, a much-touted precautionary drink for what's coming. One of our group says that she definitely gets altitude sickness above 7,000 feet, and has started taking some pills which are now producing some small unwelcome side-effects. I guess she really wanted this trip.

Short flight to Cusco (100,000 population). The airport is small with lots of gaudy-colorful stalls and signs displaying tour options. Our bus is relatively large and comfortable. We meet the local guide—Angel. (I know we are high up, but angels?) A map is handed out for Angel's explanation of our itinerary during this stay (last 2 days will be back in Cusco itself). We now begin the departure through the somewhat level-base town with suburbs that rise off the floor display reaching up into a sea of mountain-side shanty-quality adobe houses, close together, uniformly roofed with red tiles. Angel uses the word "squatters" to say how these residents migrated here from farms looking for a better life but finding themselves still trapped in poverty.

Today is Sunday on which market day is observed, and we see some cases of this on our drive through Cusco. The streets have mostly a rough cobblestone base. Some statues—a very large one near the airport to commemorate an Inca king—the Alexander-the-Great of Inca times, says Angel. Street sides are lined with adobe walls that are stitched with house stalls with small doorways. Some stretches are exhibiting many kinds of fruit for sale although the street has a residential, rather than market, look. Along the way there is a surprising number of dogs and not-surprising multitude of children. This street shows poverty—some garbage piles, a make-shift tiny concrete soccer field (in play), occasional cow, pig, sheep, donkey—tethered in all cases to a house front or side (when there are "sides"). We climb up and out of the Cusco valley into the arms of the Andes. At a point above the city we stop, get out to view the long low-lying sweep of Cusco in the valley. A moving sight, having heard and read of it so often, aware of it as a special place in Peru, a cradle of an ancient vibrant civilization (actually, several—the Incas were "recent," and very advanced and gifted).

We leave Cusco to ascend long, hairpin-curving roads to the higher altitude village of Chinchero for a visit on our way to the Sacred Valley—Urubamba Valley—and the city of Urubamba, where altitude will decrease. For the time being though, it's up and up to surely what must be the top of the world. I think of Himalayas and Shangri La pictures and films I've seen. It's a rising up into a sphere that is light in both senses of the word. The scenes sweep and spread like terrestrial clouds that have no sense of boundary. But this is not the top. As we round more curves the upward climb of the Andes continues to unfold as though it's an endless journey.

Into the village of Chinchero—cobblestone streets lined with adobe buildings—rather quiet and seemingly not much occupied. We dismount the bus for a short walk to a small factory/shop to see the weaving process. Before reaching the shop we encounter a few children eagerly trying to sell us postcards, and several women in traditional dress. The shop itself is small-scale, as are its women-folk inhabitants. There are some 10-12 women ranging in age from, let's say, seniors to teenage girls who work at the weaver's trade. They are authentically dressed in Peruvian highlands style which we've seen pictured many times. Beautiful hats—sort of inverted bowls with up-curved rims perched atop a full head of black hair, colored deep red, with fresh flowers neatly nestled in the top center, a definitive flash of panache. The hair comes out the back underside of the hat in two long braided bands which are then joined at their ends, forming a kind of inverted arch-line on the back. Lovely Indian faces that have ready smiles, but also, when not smiling, are framed in a solemn, blank, staring, patient look. The clothes seem (and are, I think) multi-layered—handsome woven wools multi-colored in patterns. They are quite short in statue—their hat-tops barely reach my shoulders—and stocky.

Our guide, Angel, is well-known here apparently and serves well as MC to move a show-and-tell demonstration of sheep, Llama and Alpaca wools, cleaning (by dipping into liquid from a special source, a liquid also used as shampoo), spindling, dying, weaving. All of the Peruvian women-in-a-row are busily, continuously working their top-spinning spindles whereby the wool is held up higher by the left hand while the right hand fingers/plucks extrudingly the fuzzed-up wool into a string that winds around the spining spindle, somehow also held and operated in the right hand. With wool string on a spool, the next stage is weaving.

Talk about various kinds of wool (and a touch-it pass-around opportunity), sources of dyes—all natural and ancient materials and processes.

We have a buying opportunity, as this establishment serves both as a shop-with-goods-for sale and a factory where weaving etc takes place. A lot of blankets, table cloths, belts, gloves, scarfs, etc. I select a 10" high doll, in part because it looks exactly like a 10-year old girl standing in our midst in front of me with her worker-mother. I have her picture (with permission). I tell them it's a gift: *es para mi nieta quien es viente-dos meses* (it is for my granddaughter who is twenty-two months old—and it seems they understand, that I said it sufficiently ok, but I'm sure they would "seem" to understand if I had said I have a fetish for Andesean dolls, and would have smiled). (I have the pleasure of having Edie Jane's beautiful smile right here in my head.) I also buy a Llama-wool "throw" something (as in "throw rug"?)—a round rug-like wool collage of a Llama and a peasant, inlaid in several colors of Llama wool, about 20" in diameter. I bought it for a very good reason which never surfaced in my brain, not even later. Very rich, soft Peruvian, and right colors. Others are buying. I walk to the bus which has moved to a spot near a sizeable Sunday-morning market. A large (for a small village) size gathering for visiting and gossip-swapping.

From Chinchero we go down. The bus is smooth and quiet. A long descending ribbon road slowly snaking into the embrace of the valley. Dramatic but soft scenes of mountain meadows, grids of small cultivated fields, flowers unveiling themselves in here-and-there patches, wide-distant vistas of cultivated geometries of shades of green—potatoes, beans, small sheep-herds grazing. Quite a beautiful glide along rich upland meadows over-watched by background peaks nestled under light-tossing clouds. The bus continues its glide into a gorgeously-designed valley of rolling hills, cuts of ravines and animals and stretches of astonishing vistas. There seems always to be the distant mountain-backing of a mist-ghosted dark Andean presence.

I could probably write a book about this 45-minute bus ride from Chinchero to Urubamba City. How much I've not told you about.

I see now the valley floor of Urubamba City, down there—many square miles of flat, flat valley floor, gridded with streets and street-side rows of adobe houses and shops. Talk by Angel about the recent heavy rains, mudslides and damage. It's quite evident (though not prominent) in Urubamba, through which the substantial and rapid-current Urubamba River is rushing. It has been at a rampage level, and mudslides were common. The heaviest rains in a long long time. This is what washed away a section of railroad tracks between here and Machu Picchu that canceled the two days we would have spent in Machu Picchu (not far from this spot—about 50 miles, and the train to Machu Picchu passes through Urubamba on its way).

We go to a restaurant for a 3p lunch. A lovely, river-side tucked-away spread of colonial-style architecture and materials of wood and stone. Very picturesque. Large buffet spread with characteristic heavy wooden tables and chairs. The long day, late hour, and (undoubtedly) the altitude have conspired to quell my appetite, so I eat a few spoons of soup, sample one bite of chile rellenos, and call it quits. I walk about the grounds, including a visit with 2 raucous self-satisfied parrots.

Next we go to a ceramics factory. We see inside its walled-in array of buildings, courtyards and walkways, a cage with a monkey and a rabbit, 2 large parrots, rooms for ceramic-making in progress, a pen for 4 adult and one child Llamas, intently munching a stringy green straw as though our presence is irrelevant. I am not much impressed by the shop of ceramic wares, although obviously it has art, color, shape, culture, enterprise. I cannot help but recall the fabulous displays of ancient ceramics and textiles (and stone and metal objects) at the Museo Larco in Lima.

On to the Sonesta Pasada del Inca hotel in Yuca, about 15 minutes from Urubamba, nestled (aren't they all) within the lofty dark green mounds of Andesean mountains, where the tops play peek-a-boo with gossamer clouds of mist that moves in breezy swaying.

For the evening I feel spent and not hungry, so I relax in my room, no writing, no reading. I watch TV news and an absurd movie of knights and maidens and jousting. I've never done that kind of thing before.

I'm up early, a passing grade on my breakfast appetite and now I sit in the garden outside the restaurant in the midst of a few adobe and wood buildings with rich stucco colors, trees and mountains rising just across the space. I have the feeling that I can reach my arm somewhat and touch them.

The Sonesta Pasada del Inca is a cluster of buildings interlaced with walkways, fountains (*sin aqua*), willows and other trees, upstretched cactus "trees," benches, flowers and embracing light, clouds and green mountain sides. Its former life was a monastery.

At 930a we depart for Ollantaytambo at the bottom end of the Sacred Valley (next stop would be Machu Picchu, if we could) and, next to it, the Inca mountainside temple that's an Inca stonework destination for visitors. The drive is descending downstream alongside the strong current.

Urubamba River, through the city of Urubamba, traveling into the narrowing Sacred Valley that will end at the temple, about 20 miles or so further on. More sweeping (but closer range, and sweeping steeply upward) cultivated fields of corn, animals, etc. The mountainside becomes steeper and more rocky, with some sections of sheer vertical rock cliffs. The valley is disappearing but not before we reach the short climb to the village of Ollantaytambo. The bus parks in the small square having much construction material and activity.

We begin along a gradual ascending cobblestone street lined by high walls consisting to a substantial degree of original Inca masonry—large mortar-less cut stones. In Inca times each block was divided into 2 parts, each part surrounded by the high wall with only one high stone-constructed portal into each part (at opposite sides of the block). The interior of each part comprises dwelling places and courtyards, maybe for one or more families or clans. The walled blocks are divided by long very narrow streets with no wall entrances. The extent seems to be, say, 8 blocks distance in each direction for each street-grid line. When Spaniards came they wanted more entrances, and got them.

We walk to about the 3rd block and have admission to a house. Through an original portal, into a small courtyard (30 x 30 feet or so), populated by a fair number of ducks and chickens, two or three lying-around dogs, 2 men sitting on a lump of ground next to a small entrance-way to a room. We enter a high threshold, small door opening (5 feet) into a dim-lit rectangle room (25 x 15 feet with 15 foot ceiling). Very cluttered, dirt floor, with 3 or 4 people, hardly noticed as they each sit in some type of doing some small thing or nothing. The family (4 or 5 people?) lives in this room. A couple (?) of bed like structures on one end, various things along the walls or ?, at one end a table along an altar-like wall with Inca religious artifacts, including an inset for 3 tomb-type skulls, a ritual doll, a display (beside the crypt inset) of 3 unborn Alpacas "suspended" one over the other (large, medium, small) with long stilt-looking legs. Related to a belief that, taken naturally (dead mother or ?) before birth they would have no after-life, so in this way (?) they have. The story has more to it, of course, but I doubt that it gets any better.

A key eye point in the room is a rather large pack of Guinea Pigs, central on the floor, kind of like a very large litter of puppies. Feeding on a type of long stringy green-leaf plant (sold in the market). You toss it to them on whims, and they go to their work of getting bigger and fatter. (Guinea Pigs are a favored "delicacy" we keep hearing.) This is a hard sadness for me personally, considering my sensitivity to the act of killing and eating things, and I'm surrounded by a barnyard (and house-floor) of cute Guinea Pigs, ducks, chickens, ready for the killing and eating. I quietly leave the group and return to the street to await their emerging through the wall-door. I buy a string of post cards from a pretty, well-dressed 12-year-old female entrepreneur—one of a small gang.

I am aware of how dirty and primitive-peasant-life this house scene is—and it seems embarassingly invasive for us tourist-gawkers to come and hear Angel's detail, full descriptions, and gawk. (I know. I know. Economics, need, consent, payment—"everybody benefits") I learn a lot—Inca religious beliefs (not expunged entirely by Catholicism—a message Angel seems eager to make), no invention of writing ever in their amazing history, a string-of-knots abacus system of numbers and information transfer, etc.

Next we re-board the bus to go to the "suburb" temple location—an awesome cobblestone plaza fronting a gated entrance to a smaller walk-ways-arranged area that is the "base" to the large-scale stone terracing ascending at about 45 degrees slope. The scale and quality of the masonry is amazing (while in the head the questions of whence, why and whither of those people). People are walking up a large stone-steps stairway to a mid-top landing, and then another stairway to the top, where a few (one in particular) mammoth stones are visible at the summit-line. I go with a few of our group to the midpoint, becoming quite aware of the altitude factor (9,000 feet?) as I ascend, step by step. Only one of us (not me) goes higher than the midpoint. From this landing the village of Ollentaytambo is visible and the valley beyond. I descend and walk to the end of the base area to see water fountains at work, water channeling from somewhere above.

Some small amount of information at this stage about the temple/fortress Inca site. It is said that the work stopped when the Spanish came. (I've read another prevailing theory that Machu Picchu [50 miles downstream] had been abandoned before the Spanish came because of devastating disease and decimating civil war which had made Machu Picchu [and projects of this nature, if any] unsustainable, which also explains why Pizarro with a relatively small number of men overcame the Incas so quickly and completely, and why he never knew about Machu Picchu. If this theory is correct, possibly this temple site work had been abandoned pre-Pizarro for the same reason.)

We board the bus for the return to the hotel, up the Urubamba River to Yucay. Along the way we stop for 30 minutes at a chicharea, a local "pub" identified by a colorful iconic flag hoisted atop a pole atop the building. When hoisted, the pub's open, etc. Inside we are given a demonstration by a woman of how the chichi drink is made from 3 types (out of a huge range) of corn—first it's fermented in water, then dried, then boiled, then drained through a filter-cloth into a 3 foot-high vat/jar. From the vat she dips the light yellow frothy fluid into a large glass, larger than a beer mug, their regular drinking-glass size. A second vat contains a similar drink, but strawberry colored because it's made as a mix of a drink from fermented strawberries and chichi. We are given tastes of each. Quite drinkable. The chichi is kind of bland; the strawberry one is kind of sweet. To this indulgence are served a corn hors d'oeuvre—it looks sort of like peanuts but in fact it's kernels of corn, roasted, quite good.

    The chichi has about a 2% alcohol content, so not an intoxication issue. Men drink it a lot during their work in the fields. Children drink it. The men assemble after work in chichareas—much like the pub practices in the U. K., and bars in the U. S., but without the intoxication. It's not exportable—confined to this mountain valley region. It's made daily as needed, and does not have much shelf life. It's fresh and refreshing.

    Lunch at the hotel, depart at 3 for a market in Urubamba, near the town center. A 1-block walk. The building is a large full-block size, 2-story-high ceiling interior. The floor is quite dirty (seems to be a dirt floor). Rows and rows of various "produce"—corn, potatoes, vegetables, cheese (many things not recognizable) on display racks, on the floor, sometimes spilling out, variously watched over by mostly women, here and there a few children are playing. Angel does a lot of explaining—what's what, how the market works, etc. Dogs, chickens, pigeons move about freely. I'm struck by how unclean and unpleasant the whole business is. So I'm not dwelling on this. I do notice and dwell a little at one substantial stall with a well-dressed young woman attending, which is beautifully and cleanly displayed, a wide variety of vegetables and other interesting items. It's remarkable that this one outstanding example exists, and has not "caught on." Evolution, why are you so slow?

TUESDAY, MARCH 2

Leave the hotel at 9a for the drive back up the Urubamba River Valley road to Cusco, to take about 1½ hours. We will re-trace our route from Cusco taken on Sunday.

As we exit Yucay I decide to use my Bose music earphones while watching exquisite mountains and valley scenes stream past my bus window. The Yucay street scene is a string of roadside shabbiness— a few men here and there, a stack of old tires against a wall (tires, that is—not men who are old tires stacked against a wall), rickshaw buggies parked possibly for repairs (to my mind comes the phrase from equestrian lexicon: rode hard and put away hot too many time), untidy dangling village streets. We begin to ascend. One after another adobe hut/house, here and there are piles of something, a pathway entrance to a path to somewhere, overhead wires strung in sagging down-looping curves from pole to pole.

I click my Bose on a selection of a few Corsican folk songs I acquired when Amy and I were there a few years ago because I'm beginning to be reminded of that day we took a drive out of Porto into the wonderland of rocky geology mountains, where we encountered a herd of goats being taken to lowland pastures (stopping traffic), as we meandered along the fun, thin strips of up-and-down curving, dipping, rising roads and roadside places, mountain scenes where the earth itself joins in the rip-open of color, encountering as well a pack of wild boars, not even aware that they are wild. Now I see Urubamba stretched out down below like it is flat-ironed along the valley floor while a haunting Corsican song plays in my head which also is seeing the enfolding mountain peaks arise studded across the valley's far side, mingling up high with cotton-candy light/dark clouds allowing rich azure pieces to break into the sky scene. Like I saw on the Sunday downstream trip, stunning scenery of green large fields of wild tiny yellow flowers, neatly laid-out cultivated fields, occasional sights of people working, etc. Visual and auditory music.

Ascending high over Urubamba City, we make an overview stop to stand and marvel.

Our arrival in Cusco involves descending (although the elevation rose from 9,000 or so feet at Yukay to 11,000 feet at Cusco) into a large relatively level expanse of Cusco City in a valley cradle. (I'm guessing a little in my altitude statements. It's true that Cusco is 11,000 feet and that Machu Picchu is about 8,000 feet, so descending from Cusco to "near" Machu Picchu, that is, Urubamba, Yukay and Ollantaytambo, would come down to, say, 9,000 feet, more or less.)

Our first stop is the Cathedral at the central square (Plaza de Armes). We have to change from the big bus used for the Valley trip to a smaller van-type as required by Cusco traffic law. Within a few blocks there are several (17?) major churches but the Cathedral (no modifying name) is pre-eminent. It was constructed on the site of the palace of the Inca Viracocha (the conqueror's right of out-with-the-old, in-with-the-new), begun about 1540 (?) and taking 94 years to build. Architects, craftsmen, artists and artisans were brought by the Church from Spain and elsewhere who worked, and also trained indigenous people. As we saw, the indigenous artisans and artists creatively blended their religions and world-view into the icons and decorations. The picture of Catholicism experienced some subtle and not-so-subtle transformation. For example, a large painting of The Last Supper hanging prominently in the Cathedral shows Jesus and the disciples around a table with a roasted Guinea Pig on a plate in the center (referring only to one "altering" aspect of the painting). The Cathedral is opulent and awesome, a huge and successful aggregation of Spanish, Catholic and Inca monument-making in the 16th century in Cusco, Peru. How does one absorb incoming awareness of such happenings on earth?

Next our smaller (but ample) vehicle took us to the Museo de Arte Pre-Colombino for a 1-hour tour of pre-Columbian artifacts. The works are on loan from the larger Larco museum in Lima which I visited on my first day in Lima. It is, therefore, for me, a re-visit, but very enjoyable. I wander through, marveling at how much the imagination of these successive pre-Columbian (Inca and pre-Inca) cultures had been released. I allow myself to think about how my own imagination at home might feel this inspiration, and use it, in my sculpting ambitions. We'll see.

Next, a good lunch, and then check in at Liberadator Hotel—a really pleasant, tasteful hotel. Free for the afternoon until a lecture at 6p at the hotel.

I stroll to the Plaza de Armes overlooked by the Cathedral—a large block-size park with a fountain in the center. Benches situated in numerous places, beds of flowers, etc. bounded by streets and on the opposite side of the streets are rows of shops. Walking about in Cusco is to swim through street vendors of all ages selling all kinds of wares (artifacts, water colors, CDs, sweaters, religious artifacts, Inca artifacts, etc., etc.) "No" or *"No, gracias"* are not audible words, and one develops strategies, such as zombie-walking on. I yield to a 13-year-old (say) with CDs when I say (in my impeccable Spanish) but I can't listen to them. And she says, by action: oh, yes you can, as she pulls out a CD player with earpieces and I say ok, *yo escucho*. It works well as I stand with her and listen. 3-5 other vendors gather close (they smell blood). Together we scroll through some sample songs and I say *Yo quiero que este. Un otro?* So, another. *Yo quiero que este.* Another? *No mas gracias. Bastante.* I pay (not much). Next, a sweater woman. It is $15, so I pay, either to buy the sweater or to give her the business. Next, a young man with very small water colors, and I try to shake him. But he's too charming, as I walk, he at my side, into the plaza. His name is Joel. He just graduated from high school in Chinchero 40 miles away (I was there) and he travels back and forth each day. He's studying art and would like to go to the University in Lima and study architecture. He has some English, as you would suspect since I would not have gotten all of this information (and more) with my Spanish alone. So I bought 3 for $10. I then found the Irish bar across the plaza (upstairs) that I had noticed earlier through the window of the van. It has the real feel. In fact I have a brief chat with a lad from Dublin, sitting on a bar stool watching a replay of Ireland's recent win over England in rugby. I have a Guinness in Cusco! Then it's time to get back to Liberadator for the lecture.

Our group along with another group (larger, Canadian) gather in a small lecture room for a power-point presentation by well-qualified (National Geographic background, I read) Peter Frost. He gives a thumbnail overview of Peruvian history, cultures, geography, etc, to zero in on Machu Picchu—its story and views of its *raison d'etre* (pardon my French), mysteries, construction, layout, abandonment, and discovery. Peter gives an excellent picture of traveling the Inca Trail. There were several "trails" for getting to Machu Picchu, but one is pre-eminent. It takes 4 days hiking, carrying what you need, but in doing so, making use of attendants to do the carrying. Advance arrangement, etc, are required, of course. The overriding point is that the "experience" of taking the trail, the ascending and descending, the vistas—all amalgamate into a spiritual high, even apart from reaching Machu Picchu itself. It's too much to tackle here. It was a religious place, and Peter gives good descriptions of the religious and world-views that would motivate the Incas to make this supreme creation, and we could see the enormous ingenuity, skill, imagination and attainment that is Machu Picchu. More opportunity for our group to bemoan our lack of access to visit the real thing. Like Moses, we were allowed to come close but were stopped short of the promised land. I bought 2 books from Peter, wiped the tear from my eye, and joined our group for dinner in the hotel.

Again, the Liberadator is so pleasantly done in color, material, appointments, and the dining experience is very good.

Wednesday, March 3

At 9a we meet in the lobby to go across the street to the Conventa y Musea de Santa Catalina built at the beginning of the 1600s on top of an important Inca religious site. (Cusco was the capital, and the heart, of importance in Inca, so nothing was spared in creating what they sought, which was religion driven. Having said that, I note that I've read that the principle reason for this extensive enclosed facility was to sequester the Inca Emperor's chosen Virgins of the Sun. (It seems that when men of mankind achieve a strategy to empower themselves with religious authentication and perhaps deification, they somehow add on a touch of my-chosen-women collection.) The Catholic Spaniards (or Spanish Catholics?) did their usual change-it-to-Catholic grand strokes, and converted (what was not destroyed or built over) into the great masonry structures to housing for monks and, next building, nuns, as well as chapels and other religious accommodations. From Angel we get information in front of us about how to know an authentic Inca wall masonry, and a pop quiz in a couple of places. It helps to sharpen the eye and appreciation for masonry skills and engineering that are probably second to none in the history of the world. The museum expresses a strong sense of old Inca and old Catholic—modern-day Cusco efforts to preserve the past and tourism.

As we are in the museum the large courtyard gives us evidence of an on-going very hard rain. When we emerge, however, it has mostly ceased. Our guide, Angel, informs us that our next 2 destinations on the edges of Cusco have been canceled due to mudslides on our route. (What? Again?) He and Gary make the arrangement with a local Inca priest for a demonstration. Nevertheless, this cancellation gets a partial reprieve, and we proceed in our bus, with our newly acquired Inca priest aboard, to travel out of Cusco to Sacsayhuaman (pronunciation: sounds like: sexy woman), touted as the greatest and nearest-to-Cusco Inca ruins, with extraordinary Inca architecture and monumental stonework. Thankfully, this part of our tour is preserved.

It's monumental in several respects. One is the size of some of the in-place building block stones. One large one at ground level, about 12 feet high, 6 feet wide (width and amount below ground is not known) is estimated to be 120 tons (if I remember correctly). I will not take the time to describe. Guidebooks are available.

In a nearby shop with weaving men at work, and plenty of merchandise, we are given a closed-area corner to sit in a semi-circle to witness the priest's ceremony. Our priest (Angel explains) has gone through levels of qualification episodes. He is a commonly-clad typical Peruvian male. He sits in a chair with a small blanket spread at his feet. He starts an arrangement with small flowers and has a collection of small green leaves on which he blows his breath, and chants.

I don't want to take the time, and you don't have the time, for me to word you through the slow, detailed hocus-pocus invoking of leaves, symbols, types of seeds, etc, etc. Each of us is given 3 small coca leaves (3 means "up above," where we are now, and beneath the ground—a favorite concept used in many ways in Inca religion) to chew or just hold while meditating. At the end (1 hour) he has a small pile of various ingredients, folds a cloth slowly and neatly around it (to bag it) and ties it expertly with a string.

If this were an actual Inca ceremony, it would be burned before the group, spirits would ascend, etc. In our case we have the assurance that he will dutifully perform the ceremony on our behalf, which will benefit us. Next (surprise?), he briefly shows us that he has a few items he would be willing to sell to us. I cannot simply "dismiss" out of hand this kind of conduct (like the shaman ceremony in the Amazon) because mankind in many ways indulges in numerous forms in various kinds of so-called belief systems. This topic is huge. Our Inca priest is simply a specific transparent simpleton instance. Like my question for the Amazon people—who are these people?

    I'll say a few words here. The Cusco experience is very warm and agreeable. I have a few interactions (apart from "people watching") and all are entirely pleasant. Attractive smiles, pleasing features, friendly attitude, etc. I like what I see. We go to lunch, our last "together" meal. A nice upstairs restaurant at Plaza de Armes, with no other customers. A band and dancers entertain us. I really enjoy this and them, and 2 pisco sours. Seven band members with a variety of instruments, including, of course, various sizes and configurations of flutes (other names refine the global word "flute"). The band is good, some songs that exude the haunting mystical Peruvian flute sound (I buy one of their CDs, of course.) Dancers are 3 female, 3 male, several sets (each set with a different traditional stylized Peruvian costume). Lovely people, great faces complete with beautiful eyes. The last performance suddenly presents a young woman in front of me beseeching me to join her on the dance floor. Who could resist her? Fortunately 2 other males of us, and 3 females, get the same invitation. What a lively show we put on, and I begin to notice the 11,000 feet altitude. Finally, not a second too soon, the music stops, and I hear thunderous applause, and I get to sit and breathe.

We are bused to the hotel with announcements to be on the bus for the airport at 9a tomorrow morning. Most of tomorrow for me will be travel, including the departure from Lima at 1245, arriving Houston 615a. It's called fly-by-night.

And, in effect, for my trip to the Amazon and Cusco and the Sacred Valley, the music has stopped.

The next day (Thursday), we go to the Cusco airport, fly to Lima, transfer to the Sonesta el Olivar Hotel, where I check in to a room. By this time it's late afternoon (the Cusco-Lima flight was delayed). I meet my driver at 9p, say goodbye to Gary (the others are in their rooms etc), and go to the airport. Departure at about 1a for Houston, arriving at about 630p. A pleasant flight, mostly sleep.

When the Amazon Basin is mentioned, or Cusco, or Sacred Valley, I will know a lot more about that than I did prior to this trip. It was an experience desired and fulfilled.

As a post-script, I will share with you my effort within a week of leaving Peru to bring my thoughts to a distillation which, for me, is often cast as a poem:

Ancient Peru

                         where are you?
Shrouded in the dark of no written language
and all your pre-Pizarro ruins are detritus
for us to wonder and guess at what you were.

Through five thousand years in pockets of time and place
in knitted groups you hunted and farmed and fished
and built, adding religions and art to your riches.
Why did you do this, religions and art?
You did it so well in imaginations that romped and played,
liberated like your multitudes of birds in your wild winds
of your endless coastal plains, your Andes and your Amazon.

We rummage our mental sticks in the ash piles
of cultures that took a wrong turn, or got fated away;
our eyes made wide to see the Inca civilization,
slaughtered by Pizarro and the likes of him
who came for gold but did not see the gold before their eyes.

YEATS POETRY FESTIVAL: SLIGO, IRELAND (2010)

Friday, July 24[10]

Arrive in Dublin early in the day and go to Temple Bar Hotel in the Temple Bar section—pedestrian-dedicated narrow cobble-stone streets and pubs and shops and restaurants, a part of the heart of Dublin. The very popular band, U-2, is playing this weekend at the big stadium (they say a hundred thousand fans will attend), so Dublin is filled with band-going fans, filling up the hotels. (Temple Bar was a lucky one-room-left find by me on the internet, after several other choices failed.) During the day I enjoy very much strolling around this heart of Dublin area, Temple University, St. Stevens Green, Shelborne Hotel (where I have spent nights on several visits), etc. I remember a time when I had delicious kippers for breakfast in Shelborne's dining room, and inquire. No kippers. (It turns out, kippers are not as ubiquitous as in the old days.) Where to find? I receive a reference that is a taxi ride away, which I do, to a small competent seafood restaurant, and have kippers because I'm in Ireland and I like kippers. Continue after lunch strolling along the Liffey River and soaking in the sense of Dublin. Light, simple dinner at Temple Bar Hotel before going to Abby Theater, which is a must for me when in Dublin. (I fail to note the name of the performance for this journal—it is a comedy period piece, old chestnut, pulling out all of the costumes and stagey acting style, very silly, but by the second act I begin to limber up and almost laugh a little.) Afterwards I enjoy strolling around the loud, crowded and lively partying scene of Temple Bar U-2 phenomenon. I note that every female in Dublin wears blue jeans. I'm thinking thoughts about young Irish people, how it's changed since my first trip in the early 60s, a strong sense of "modern" has arrived, and I'm sort of experiencing the "generation gap" although I'm quite comfortable with the young people I'm beholding. Soon I brave it and wade my way up to one bar to have a Guinness but then head for my room: the young-crowd jubilation is too overwhelming for me.

Saturday, July 25

My train to Sligo will be at about mid-day, so I have morning time. I decide on going to Trinity College Dublin campus for viewing, but especially the museum. A beautiful day, a beautiful campus, and lovely old buildings and big and bigger statuary commemorations of noteworthy historical personages. A good use of two hours.
Next I'm on the train from Dublin to Sligo. So many thoughts. The fabulous scenes streaming by as a dream would stream a poem about this train ride in Ireland just completed. In the next seat, a little boy growing up right now, a woman across the aisle reading and writing, the low clouds dark and light puffy in the light. Little gatherings now and then of cows, of sheep, some of horses, all busy consuming the lush grass which anyway spreads like ancient yeast thickly coating the Emerald Isle. Stubby trees, hedge rows, banks and borders lace around quilting the green. The train is clean smooth quiet and now and then glides into a station in silence where Irish folk in travel garb tend their business of coming and going then the train pausing at the station for only one or two breaths. The train moves along again as much as ease can be. Seeing scenes, a house, a narrow road, there a string of old stone wall and another over there. Now as Sligo must be coming soon the horizon is showing higher and higher hills that serve to magnify the grandness of how the earth is made.

Arriving in Sligo 220p, quietly into a small station filled with people and the parking area is a traffic jam, a small area. My first move to a taxi works in the confusing scene. Then to the Glasshouse Hotel.

Message from Maureen that she will arrive late and will see me the next day (Sunday). After settling in, I go to the Yeats headquarters building (lovely old building directly across Hyde Bridge Street from the Glasshouse) to register. Meet Jan from San Francisco, Martin from Sligo, Maura at registration with whom I had emailed. Get the info. Go a short walk to Keohanes' Book Store (turns out, the book store *de rigueur* for Sligo and the Yeats Festival) for recommended Yeats book of poetry.

First I go wrong but a young man at a music store sat me right with politeness and clarity, a typical encounter with an Irishman, quite warming, as I'm reminded from many trips to Ireland. The bookstore is an authentic Irish bookstore thriving on its pride to be what it is. Back to Glasshouse and a Guinness at a table beside the roaring river (the Garavogue) flowing at the foot of the Glasshouse, complete with swans.

I sit and read the packet of information about the Yeats Festival (YF) and do some editing of my poem written on the train (*Train to Sligo*), helped by the Guinness. The Glasshouse is on the spot on which a mill once stood, with waterwheel, at one time owned by Yeats's grandfather. Its interior is now a gaudy orange and black with lots of glass, as the name implies, tending well its business of hoteliering. Later, a reception and dinner to initiate the Festival at City Hotel at 730. Roughly 150 attendees from many countries.

By chance good-fortune James Freeley sits next to me. Eight at the table. Introductions. James and I hit it off with easy talk. He is from Durham, England but originated from Ireland, a shift due to his job, many years ago. He has 3 sons. His wife died last November, the same month of Amy's death, which bonded us even more. His experience much like mine—hard but here we are.

After dinner a chance bump into Larry French from Toronto but with Irish lineage. He had a family reunion in Dublin and Galway just before YF. Lives now in Switzerland and Toronto. We go to a bar for 2 rounds of Bushmill. Agree to meet next day for lunch at noon to have a mini-workshop of our poems. Should be interesting. Back to Glasshouse at 12 and bed.

Sunday, July 26

After sleeping well I awake at 615 and take a walk along the Garavogue River (used to be called Sligo River), a fulsome flowing body of dark water. Returned in 45 minutes, shower, breakfast in hotel (looking out on the Garavogue River and the swans). Called Maureen at 1030 (not knowing how late she arrived by car, but I wanted to give her the choice of joining James, Larry and me for lunch and poetry at the Southern Hotel at 1130). We walk to the Southern (where James and Larry reside) and meet.

We sit together with wine when Larry unveils from somewhere underneath his coat a bottle and glasses. We chat briefly getting Maureen introduced then begin a rotation of sharing poems and handing out copies when available, and reading aloud. I had made copies of mine at the Glasshouse for handout including the "*Dublin to Sligo*" poem just written yesterday. Then lunch.

Quick walk to Glasshouse, Maureen and I, then to Hawk's Well Theater, a main venue for YF events, for the opening remarks. Then everyone boards buses for a trip for scene viewing, including a view of Ben Bulben's Head, then to Drumcliffe Church (Episcopal) for an evening song service, running late, then outside viewing of Yeats' grave and headstone. As Yeats commanded in a poem, his epitaph reads:

> Cast a cold Eye
> On Life, on Death.
> Horseman Pass By

Very moving, to be at the grave of so great a poet, in his land (2 senses). I gleaned more insight into this enigmatic epitaph. A version (before being revised out) had another line (first line), which was: *Draw rein, draw breath* (which has a rhyme with *death*, obviously). So, (and here begins the speculation) he envisioned a horseman riding by, pausing to gaze at the gravesite. Also I read that his mind was in the time when horses and landed gentry were the upper, ruling class, and that his emigrant grandfather, though very successful financially, always felt that he did not "make it" into that class, thus bestowing a kind of "the unattained" aura on "the horseman" who would ride by. His great grandfather was rector of this church, and a thumbnail of Yeats's relationship with Sligo is in this footnote.[11] This year is the 70th anniversary of Yeats's death in 1939, and the 50th anniversary of the Yeats Poetry Festival.

The church is small and beautiful. The setting is bucolic, with much of its border being its old old cemetery, but—in nearby proximity—a large parking lot due to tourists and a site for a tearoom and tourist office. We have off-and-on showers for our outing, beautiful country to drive through, and then head back to Sligo, just in time to change and board the buses again to Cromleach Castle for a big dinner treat.

Maureen, James, Larry and I hook up for the Cromleach event. Cocktails, a good dinner, a few speeches, including brief remarks by Seamus Heaney. (He and his wife were seated in the next row in front of Maureen, James and me at the Hawks Well Theater opening meeting. It was a feeling to be in his presence.) At dinner I had conversations with Maureen Murphy on my left, a Yeats scholar from a Long Island School (name?) and a speaker at the YF. Very late bus trip back to Sligo (about 40 minutes drive), arriving Glasshouse about 130a. It's late; this is Ireland.

Monday, July 27

(Due to lack of free moments, I missed writing contemporaneously about some of this day, so some of what's written below for this day contains catch-up written 2 days later.) The routine is established on this first regular day. Lectures at Hawk's Well Theater, a short walk from Glasshouse. (Everything's a short walk in Sligo.)

Lectures are at 930 and 1115 with a 30-minute break between. This means that the second lecture ends at 1230 if it ends on schedule but seldom does. There is a 110p poetry reading at the Methodist Church so you see we have 40 minutes at best (or 20 or 10) to have lunch along the 10-minute walk through "down town" to the church.

The poetry reading is about 1 hour, bringing us to 210. Maureen's drama class is from 230 – 6 or 630, so she is immediately committed for the afternoon. I have a poetry seminar at 430 – 6, so I have 2 hours or so.

Having made the big decision to buy a red jacket at Penney's for 15 Euros (due to my failure to pack a jacket, and daytime temperatures are typically low to mid 60s, and showers occur), I proceeded to the Yeats Memorial Building (YMB), went inside to confirm that my seminar is at the same time (430) and same place (YMB library) each day, and it is. I ask 2 lovely young girls my question about the time and place of the seminar. As I suspect, they are not on the staff but step up with Irish warmth to help me readily, and go with me to a place to get the answers. I bump into James who is buying a Yeats poster to take home, and I am about to do the same when I have the thought—where would I put it? I have pictures stacked in closets, begging for walls, so I pass.

Now for an excitement. I cross the street to enter the Glasshouse which as you recall is situated on Hyde Bridge Street, next to the bridge over the Garavogue River, where directly below the window of my 4th floor room the river is a roaring rapids of arresting cascading of water and sound (the flow that was funneled through a sluice to drive the mill's waterwheel that's no longer there). A misty rain is in the air under low-banking clouds, variegated light and dark. I should say, rain is in the "wind" because as I cross the street the wind is whipping at a stimulating blow, tossing the blonde hair of a young woman across the street dressed sleekly in a black top and hip-hugging pants walking in a way that only women can walk, and I heavy in the traffic jam of my mind, and mindful incidentally of the traffic on the street, filled to my brim with the senses of the surroundings. Wet wind and roaring stream, percolating street of Sligo Ireland where the moment seems to me to be so much more than just right. It is not too much to say exhilarating.

The grand idea occurs to me, and grows in my mind as I cross Hyde Bridge Street to the Glasshouse in the mist and wind and river roar, that I will buy a pint of Guinness and take it to my room (with which I sit right now looking down on the cascading river just beneath my window, which I open to enhance the sounds of the tumbling water). I ask at the bar (through which I conveniently must pass on the way to the elevator) if I am allowed to take a pint of Guinness with me to my room and she says I don't see why not. So it is done, midst 2 other kind approaches of waiters soliciting my needs. (One young waiter asks me if I have had a Guinness before, and I give a look of pensive pause and say: 17,344 times.)

So here I am. I would like to say: all is right. But I must inject with self-conscious reluctance that, while shopping for the jacket, I thought of Amy who so often was at my side when I made clothing purchases for myself and I leaned on her for this but now I'm on my own. I think of her with every breath in my mind it seems. When I enter the hotel room she flits across my brain like a sprite as I do the thises and thats of living in a hotel room which she and I did together countless times.

Now it's time to go to my Yeats seminar—an hour and a half with direct immediate attention to the poems of W. B. Yeats, led by the well-known and highly regarded Helen Vendler of the Harvard faculty. Delving into Yeats this way is awesome. He is so unbelievably good, and having a teacher of such excellence, and fellow students who've come because of the love of poetry and Yeats's poetry. While I have read and re-read a number of his poems and know something about him and his poetry, my awareness of how much there is that I don't know is increasing in leaps. We do the poem with a long title about a wealthy man who was foolishly (in Yeats's view) placing "show me" conditions on a gift. Then "The Dolls," then "The Magi" in this session. At closing Helen made very good comments about the value and fecundity of language in man's journey. I start writing a note after the others have left, and she and I are alone. She asks what I'm writing, and I answer I'm making a note on a theme that I have in the works, that is, how today we struggle puzzlingly, in befuddlement and wonderment, and we have language, but what about man before language, his plight then. She and I shared comments on the cave paintings in France (which we both have visited), and a nice discussion.

Five of us have dinner in the bar of the Glasshouse, leaving in time to go to the Hawk's Well to hear Seamus Heaney read at 830 after which there is a gathering at a local venue for mixing and drinking. So to the Glasshouse and to bed at 1130 or so. This is a typical day. No slack time (except I get 2 hours before my seminar which seems less since I often have a chore or two).

Seamus Heaney is present throughout, with his wife. Several of the other poets are also in the mix and are seen here and there, at Hawk's Well, Methodist Church, various pubs at lunch, poetry readings, breakfast at the Glasshouse, or dinner or whatever. (James and I had a chance encounter with Seamus and his wife over a Guinness in a pub—a very convivial visit.)

Seamus is a fine looking man, experiencing at about this time his 70th birthday (it was mentioned from the stage 2 or 3 times). White hair, thinning. Just under 6 feet tall (mine is 6). Seems very gentle and kindly in demeanor and speech. Reads his poems well and modestly, with that good Irish flavor. Very good poetry.[12] Very impressive man and poet.

Tuesday, July 28

Same routine. Hawk's Well 930, 2 lectures. 2nd one ended at 1p, 10 minutes before the 110 poetry reading at Methodist Church. I am not capturing the names of lecturers and poets but refer you to the program. The bags are mixed. A lot of Yeats knowledge and information. Another lecture on Yeats, Pound and Elliot, etc. Poets doing readings throughout the week generally have not been great and I continue to be distressed (a theme of mine) by how poorly many poets read their poetry. I try to take into account, when making this complaint, my distressingly poor hearing, helped a little but inadequately by my hearing aids.

Today, instead of mid-day poetry reading, there is a bus trip to Lissadell House along the coast near Sligo Bay, and along this route are many good views of Ben Bulben's Head (similar to Sunday's bus route to Drumcliffe Church). Maureen dutifully went to her drama session and misses this outing. (I need to say, the Festival has a poetry side, and a drama side, and students can elect. Maureen's class is studying Yeats's plays, and specifically planning a performance of one of them at the end of the Festival's two weeks.) James and I partnered. He is an excellent traveling companion—thoughtful, knowledgeable, courteous, alert.

Lissadell House near Rosse Point is a statement of early 20th century grand manor life in Ireland. England was where the stories and grandeur existed, so if you become an Anglo-Irish and happen to possess land and money, you could try to do it in Ireland, which is the story (in my view) of Lissadell and many other houses of landed Irish gentry of that time. We toured the house, the entry way, the ball room, the dining room, library, kitchen, servants quarters—all grand, on and on. Memorabilia portraying family scions as grand—travelers, sportsman, family, etc. The design and appointments were high quality and advanced for their time. Several ingenious "devises" installed to aid the house-functioning and comforts. There is, incidentally, currently a controversy surrounding the Lissadell House. It was purchased a few years ago and the new owners insist on the right to close it to public access (called in Irish law "right of way," i.e., the *public's* right to access). This is about to be decided by the Court. It is strange to me that a purchase could occur without the clarification of such a major question, suggesting that, as a tourist, I am not receiving important information that would explain this matter.

In any event, it is a good bus trip, great views, comfortable. Back to Sligo just in time for my 430 seminar. Afterwards, at 6, I go to the Glasshouse, passing through the bar area, and James is there. Bernie joins us. Bernie is from West Cork, attends the same seminar that I attend. I had gotten her and Maureen together, both having a West Cork presence, so Bernie has become a part of our clique. Maureen joins us at about 630, and we have dinner at the Glasshouse. Then we go to a poetry reading at the Methodist church at 830, then to a pub briefly, then home.

Friday, July 31

Two morning lectures—both had fair content but poorly delivered, especially the 2nd one—really badly delivered. Reading instead of speaking to audience, low volume, looking down at the page (never looking at the audience), too fast. Then James and I encounter Maureen as we are on O'Connell Street (a main street) walking toward The Stables (a pub that I had heard about favorably), so the 3 of us have lunch. Good. I have a pint of Guinness then a glass. James and I had decided to skip the 110 poetry reading ("local Sligo poets") as he is leaving at 4 and wants to go to Kaehan Book Store, which is also an objective of mine. We do and browse some fascinating old books. I buy 3 plus a book that I had ordered. Still waiting for 2 that I've ordered.

Then go by Maloney's (James with me) to exchange the wax coat that I recently purchased) to get brown instead of sage (which to me in most lights looks black). Noting here: obviously I've decided the red jacket from Penney's is not up to snuff, so, with James' side-bar encouragement I had bought a wax Barbour jacket (which is a popular Irish-weather style and priced a bit more than the Penney's 15 euros jacket), after sorting through styles and colors. All's well now except this last change of mind regarding color. Much ado by me about deciding to buy then switching colors. Mostly joshing through the process, as though it's important, but this may be tedious to Maureen and James. (Maureen had also gone into the shop with me briefly on our way to lunch as I sought her advice on color and she favors the brown.)

Maureen goes to her 230 drama class while James and I go to the book store, Maloney's and the YMB to see an exhibit of Jack Yeats's paintings—3 small rooms upstairs, about 18 paintings. I noted that Jack Yeats in his abstract work brought to mind dim figures such as sprites, fairies—a link to W. B.'s lean into spirits and occult.

At 630 Maureen and I walk to a nearby French restaurant (name?). Very good, small, pleasant. Unfortunately we have only 45 minutes. We make reservations for the next night. Then to the Methodist Church for 2 readings. First is by Sinead Morrissey who is to be my workshop leader on the upcoming Saturday and Sunday. She reads poorly (as in I could understand practically none of what she was saying —not using the mike competently, not making any apparent effort to project, burdened by a little girl's voice.)[13] Her poetry (in my view, limited as stated) is good.

Afterwards, Maureen and I have Irish coffee at Glasshouse and chat with Colbert Keaney and his wife Mary Morrissey (no relation to poet Sinead). Colbert is one of the YF speakers, on the faculty at the University of Cork, and lives in West Cork where Maureen has a house, and they are acquainted. After that, we retire to our rooms.

Saturday, August 1

At breakfast I am assigned one of the tables by the window that has a good close view of the Garavogue which, this morning, has a substantial collection of swans. The water tends to blackness, so the white swans almost sheen their beauty. At first, as is the routine in this breakfast room, I place my book at my place and go to the buffet for my cereal and orange juice that I have each morning. Upon returning I note that at the table next to me a couple with 2 small children (one with a screamy voice) are settling in. So I quietly pick up my book and food and the waitress follows my indication that I want another table. The point to note is that it is Sinead Morrissey, her husband and their 2 kids, so I want to make my get-away as unnoticed as possible.

I go to the workshop at 930. Although it's just across the street (in the YMB) from Glasshouse I wear my new wax (Barbour) jacket, feeling good about it, and its warmth and rain-repellant qualities. Rain is gently spraying in the light breeze (as last evening, and so often, which feels so right to me) and I have in mind that there might be a walk in the rain and cold at lunch time (which became true).

There are 15 (counting the leader) in the class, several of whom are in the Vendler seminar that ended yesterday. We have usual introductions.

I go first, having captured the important place (for me, because my hearing deficit is a real plague) on Sinead's immediate left. I only say my name and where I'm from, but all of the others elaborate on their poetry interest and experience.

At moments such as this I take notice of who will not speak clearly (again, from my perspective). One young "girl" (quite young in looks as well as the rest, probably in her 20s) all the way across the two large joined-together tables, has a wee voice of a small shy child, almost (seems to me) pathologically underpowered. So it turns out I can scarcely understand anything she says which I regret because she seems to be good at this subject. Sinead I can understand but only because of my fortuitous proximity.

Sinead begins with asking each of us to talk with the neighbor person and itemize "rules" that govern poetry (noting that rules of course can be broken). I talk with Deidra from Geneva and London (see below). When Sinead asks us to start saying the rules we have to offer, Deidra opens with the point

I had raised with her. More of a question. At the onset of a poem, what rules, since it's so difficult and quixotic to grab it (the poem being born), to know when to grab, how to grab, how to work it into traction? I don't think that any rules come forth for doing this. Rules then develop for discussion: 1. not abstractions, be specific; 2. "show" don't "tell"; 3. No clichés; 4. Economy; 5. Craft—everything should be there for a purpose.

Next, Sinead introduces the topic of Haiku, asking us to identify its rules. It is a tight rule-clutched, extremely exact form, so it serves well to carry on the topic of rules. Japanese is a syllabic language she says (and her bio tells that she had a period of teaching in Japan). So Haiku in Japanese is a special (unique) type of enterprise, doing in Japanese what it can do in no other language. Nevertheless, Haiku in English is alive and well. After we are well into defining the rules and noting that Haiku must be Haiku, I ask "why?" I'm not sure there is an answer. It may be like cutting a gem (I do not say this in class) when you know that cutting this gem in this special form yields a time-proven appeal to the eye. It's a paying attention to something that happens to want to happen when it happens right.

Next Sinead has a sort of game. Each person writes the first line of a Haiku. (Note that a Haiku has 3 lines with the number of syllables being 5/7/5, plus all the other rules: it's present tense, non-subjective, highly specific, nature-oriented, seasonal flavored, peaking in some insightful way at the close, and beautiful.) My entry for line 1 is: "ocean depth of a." Then each one passes the sheet to the person on the right, whose job is to do the 2nd (7 syllables) line. And then, the next passes, to the final "kicker" (my word) line. Then Sinead calls on two people, one after the other, to read. When read, she writes them on the "board" (a stand with a large tablet of pages so the writing can be read from across the room). Then we work it over. Where does it hit? Where does it miss? Etc. A good exercise in strict rules, strictly speaking.

Before lunch Sinead hands out a poem, a full page length, to be discussed after lunch. A kind of prose poem. By Les Douglas (never heard of him) about his 15 year old autistic son. A fantastic poem on so many levels, done with quintessential skill. It informs, and it wrings the heart with a back-light glow of love and, finally, it has a universality that grabs hold.

Lunch. I propose to the girl next door (Deidra) that we lunch together and she accepts. She wants me to lead so I suggest The Stables, a pub at which I ate yesterday but it is a good "pub" feel and not a long walk. Light misty rain is in our faces, delightfully so. A booth table. Deidra has water. I have a pint of Guinness (this choice surprises me mightily). She has "homemade" vegetable soup. I have homemade mushroom soup. (So many times in yesteryears I've had Irish mushroom soup. It is so good. Served with brown soda bread which does not need to apologize.) We chat briefly about ourselves, our background and why we're at the YF. She grew up in London but lives now in Geneva where her husband is a journalist. Has a son and daughter, both in college. She is into her PhD program in creative writing at the later-in-life stage (like my son Graham, now in a creative writing PhD program at the University of Glasgow, about whom I speak). Her school (I don't recall the name) is in London and she travels back and forth. She has a demeanor of sadness although she's pleasant. After lunch she goes to her hotel room to phone her husband. I go to Eason news store to fill my need for a writing tablet.

The afternoon session of the workshop continues 2 – 430. After discussing the poem handed out before lunch, the agenda through balance of the afternoon, and the next morning's 930 – 1230 session, is to "workshop" the poems that had been emailed in advance to Sinead. I won't dwell on this. It is a typical workshop process—the author reads a poem, another then reads the same poem, then discussion of the poem with the author remaining silent, who then comments briefly at the close. Then the next poet/poem. How the poem is selected out of the 4 or 5 each person had submitted seems a bit mixed, like, in some instances, Sinead selects, in others she seems to allow the author to select. In the end I take a peek in Sinead's stack of papers (with her consent) to see if she has selected for me. She has made extra copies for distribution of Donkey and Humor. She asks me if I have a choice (which one to read the next morning). I tell her I would let her know. But then she pulls out the Tela Kusa poem and requests that I read it because it is preeminently a "sound" poem, and I agree.

Generally the quality of the poems is quite good, and the discussions flow freely, politely and knowledgably. I am impressed compared to other workshops I've attended.

(I'll intersplice this: I'm writing this in Glasshouse bar situated next to the swan-adorned Garavogue streaming river. After the 430 close of the day's workshop, back to my room where I read a little bits and pieces. I call Maureen's room a few times but at 6p I decide to leave a note on her doorknob and adjourn to the bar for a Bushmill neat, or 2. The view from my seat toward the river has in view a couple of young persons, definitely Irish by dress and look. He is drinking Guinness, she a mixed drink. They dwell in total silence. Two young lovers? At peace? Or not? Just sitting and sort of staring. Beyond them, the river, the street across the river lined with the row of blocked and colorful structures that characterize the rowing of Sligo's streets, and many an Irish town. Above the couple sitting at the bar is the "tele," a soccer game on one, a boxing match on another, with the hotness of athletic contest. At its left is the bar, and tables spread around with strong orange (orange is the craze of Glasshouse) pull-up chairs and black tables (Halloween?). Walls on the Garavogue side are floor-to-ceiling glass which makes a great picture. There is a peculiar and acceptable glean in the way this hotel smacks its colorful presence on the somewhat drab streets by the bridge over the Garavogue, to have a gayness.

It's 7p and our reservation at the French restaurant is at 7, so I just go to my room to search for the restaurant's name to call and alert them, but Maureen shows up at this time from her drive. I am anxious to hear about her day of scenery driving since she had the day free and has a car in need of exercise. So, back to the bar now to finish my 2nd Bushmill and await Maureen's momentary appearance. We have a nice walk to the restaurant, misty and a little cold—that is (one more time) just right.

(I'm writing this the next morning, *nunc pro tunc*, as lawyers say.) The restaurant experience, the walk to it, the tolling church bell on the misty lamp-lite street of our walk, the pleasantness of the restaurant's small interior and warmness of the waiters, the ambiance of being 2 friends sharing enjoyment. Maureen has salad and salmon. I have carrot soup and lamb. I had the carrot soup the night before. Excellent. Two kinds of bread. One is a saffron color and flavor. Outstanding. Makes you want to live on bread and wine. We order a Bordeaux, the same as what we had by the glass the night before. And as though that was not enough, because it wasn't, we order a 2nd bottle of Bordeaux, a different vintage—just to compare, you understand.

A good recounting to each other of how we lived our lives that day. Maureen drove to Rosse Point and to the Lissadell House for a tour of it. Talk about its status, history, furnishings, outlook. I talk for approximately 10 hours about my 8 hours of poetry workshop and lunch with Deidra. I offer at times to stop but Maureen keeps me going with her questing interest in poetry and the mechanics of the workshop process.

We talk of what to do with our lives over the next few days of Sligo, poetry, drama workshop, the trip to West Cork (to visit for a week immediately following the YF)—shall it be Adair, or what, for a night, to visit Chris Ryan and the Scarteen hounds, and possible other friends such as Liz Barry (from her days of living in Galway and my years of annual foxhunting with the Scarteens and neighboring hunts), or

Galway where Maureen's poet sister lives, how long to make the journey to West Cork versus going straight to this place that is building in my mind? We walk back through the night streets, warmly lit for us by some friends who also have laid cobblestones and sidewalks and buildings and street lamps and moist soft air to usher us to the Glasshouse and a night's sleep and dreams by a river in an Irish town.

Sunday, August 2

At about 630 I roll out of bed and go to my table and chair by the window overlooking Garavogue's dim roar (the window is ajar to allow a breeze and sound). I have been lying for a few minutes before arising with my mind in idle when a poem seems to be forming. I proceed to write 2 poems, and insert here their *pro temp* names: "I Don't Care" and "The World is Ending Now." Then to breakfast. I pick up a newspaper from the desk at about the time I am finishing breakfast (it had not arrived when I passed the desk going to the breakfast room), thinking that I would spend a little time with coffee and Irish news. But the clatter and chatter of the breakfast room is annoying, so I ask if I can go to the nearby bar area, not now occupied, but having, in addition to quietness, views of Garavogue. She readily agrees and even offers, and I accept, to follow me to a table with a fresh pot of coffee. (They serve coffee by providing a silver serving pot so you can pour your own.) This is just an instance of the kindness and hospitableness that characterize my contacts with staff, clerks, waiters and other Irish people. A genuine delight.

However, just as I am settling in, a staff person begins to vacuum the bar area, so I take the liberty and simply carry the pot and newspaper to my room to sit at my quiet table with the marvelous view and sound. Perfect.

At 920 I cross Hyde Bridge Street to the YMB and ascend the steps to the library claiming my yesterday seat, as the others file in and find their yesterday seats.

Again, we workshop our poems. Mine is second. As I approach the moment I begin to realize that the selection of Tela Kusa was fortunate. It is a "word" poem completely, and has never been workshopped. I know that an audience might well find it very puzzling and inaccessible, so upon getting to this moment I have a case of anticipation to find out. If this class of good poets (and I will call them good poets) cannot "get it" then that will be significant information to me, and thus this is a real opportunity. I have a significant number of poems that are important to me in which there are a little or a fair amount of no-meaning words that I concoct for the sound and the "meaning" that emerges by the sound and meter in a kind of syntax—thus enriching (I think) the experience.

So I read it and then another reads it. Discussion ensues. (The new rule announced at the morning's outset was that the author is not allowed to speak until discussion ends, when he/she can say what he/she wishes.) The first commentary is a case of totally missing the picture (which engenders fear in me). "I don't know what these words are," as in, impliedly, "unless you will provide definitions I can't continue." But another speaks and she got it, saying it seems like a chant or rolling out of a ritual in a church, perhaps my private church, and she is comfortable and understanding that they are not real words (although some significant real words are sprinkled about the poem). Others climb on board and see the poem for rhythm and sound, saying compliments like "music." The form is commented on and one or two "suggestions" are made. Sinead says she loves it and I should not make a single change.

I don't know why I developed my anxiety except, probably, it was a case of stage fright. I recall that the Colby College professor with whom I did some long-distance "consulting" back in December '07 had said to me regarding this poem: "I don't like 'word-play' poems but I like this one and I think it is publishable." (Oddly, I have never submitted it for publication.) Also Kathy Beer of Inprint in Houston asked me one time to submit a poem or poems to the upcoming Texas Anthology (published in the beginning of '08), specifically requesting that I include one of my word poems. (She and I had taken Tony Hoagland's Inprint workshop together—a juried workshop in which you gain admission based on poems submitted—about 14 were admitted out of a field of some 30-plus applicants—so she had a little exposure to my poems.) I submitted 2 poems to the anthology (not Tela Kusa) and Minnie Moe Miney was accepted —itself containing a number of made-up words, beginning with the first 2 lines: "Oh Minnie Moe Miney might flu the rook, not terra not luna but una."

Anyway—the workshop proceeded to 1245 and ended. A worthwhile and enjoyable experience.

Back to Glasshouse. Maureen and I have lunch there with the previously made plan to drive to Strandhill and environs. I have a pint of Guinness and fish and chips. Excellent. Best I've ever had. Maureen has coffee and pie, since she had had a late breakfast and she is to do the driving in her rent car (a nice Mercedes).

It is a fine drive of scenery and geography. Maureen does well with driving on the wrong side of the road. It is quite an interesting place for me—just sitting and enjoying the view. For so many years in all of my and Amy's trips, I was always the driver while Amy sat and viewed. Not complaining because that's the way it had to be. Amy was not a "strong" driver and I could handle driving in foreign lands even on the wrong side. So this was a treat midst really stunning scenery.

We drive through Strandhill but do not stop. A small sea-side village. Being a 3-day holiday weekend (a bank holiday as they say in Ireland) it is a somewhat crowded scene. We drive on to Carrowmore Megalithic Cemetery, a little further on. Knocknanea Mountain is a prominent feature as we circumnavigate its base and then move on but it stays within our sight.

We spend about 1½ - 2 hours visiting the area which has "sites" scattered around with stone cairns (sites for burials or rituals). Various configurations of stones, and various stone sizes and compositions, although concentricity is the major theme. The land is very open and wide-ranging in its views. Cairns dot the landscape over a large area, much larger than the immediate sites marked on the walking map for viewing.

I won't attempt a thorough review. The cairns date from about 6300 years ago. The culture is known only sketchily. The small 2-room museum at the small entrance office has a lot of information and booklets are for sale. I buy one. The people were hunters and gatherers on land and shore side. There were rituals practiced with and about the cairns apparently but not much is known specifically. These types of ritualistic stone compositions were developed in many cultures ranging over Europe and Asia as well as all over Ireland. (Of course one knows about Stonehenge in England and its mysteries. They predate the pyramids.) I take photos here and there. One couple (Irish) offer to take a picture of us so we accept, and reciprocate. Turns out the man is a painter, just arrived to this area, with plans to do some painting.

Next door is a riding stable and arena so we stick our heads in for a few minutes. Not much going on. Apparently a riding school with summer class for foreign students. We hear some German as we enter and then inside there is a group of young French riders. Only one horse being worked, dressage-type activity in an arena with jumps.

A drive along a climbing road up Knocknanea. Sparsely studded with houses. Road wide enough for only one car, so when we meet another, one has to back up to a driveway or some nook place to allow the other car to proceed. Beautiful views although the weather is rainy with heavy clouds.

Back to Sligo, dinner and bed.

Monday, August 3

In the morning, usual routine of 2 lectures at Hawk's Well, then quick lunch, 110 poetry reading. Maureen and I renew our discussion of departure options, whether a 2-day Sligo to West Cork versus a full day's drive. I offer to do the steps to have myself qualified with her car rental company so we can share the driving but the decision came down that Maureen will be the only driver. If we take any side trips or stops we would have to spend the night somewhere en route.

Reasons and plans for side trips are mentioned above. We decide to do a one-day trip on Friday, Thus missing the Festival's last day. We decide that this will allow a brief stop at Coole Park, the site of Lady Gregory's home just south of Galway where Yeats spent so much time writing. Also by talking with her brother, Ross, on her cell phone it is arranged that we will meet at Coole Park and a picnic lunch.

In the afternoon Maureen goes to her drama class and I go to Keohanes' Book Store—my 3rd trip. Long visit with Michael Keohane. We talk several subjects as he has the inveterate Irish way of forwarding on and on through topics. His range of interests and knowledge as a bookstore owner gives him a lot of qualifications. Then I go walking. I bump into Peter from my workshop class. We are near the section called The Mall. I ask Peter if the section up the street ahead is The Mall and he says yes. He says he was born and raised on that street. He asks if he could walk with me. Of course I am delighted. A guided tour by a fellow poet who is home again for a visit, with a lot of information and things to point out. We end up along the river and then part at the time we need to get ready to go to our seminar, taught (this week) by Peter McDonald. Peter (my friend) had been in the Vendler seminar with me during the preceding week and now he and I are in the McDonald seminar this week.

Peter McDonald of Oxford is a poet (I heard him at one of the poetry readings), teacher, lecturer, and scholar. His lecture at Hawks Well on Yeats, editing, Yeats on William Blake, planning and publishing his own works, etc., was very full and very well delivered. The overarching theme of the week's seminar is to be sound and form of Yeats's poems, a good path to pursue. The class is in a building opposite Sligo City Hall on Wine Street, 3rd floor, down the hall. A kind of hotel meeting room with that kind of (think plastic-like) tables and chairs. About 12 students, with McDonald at the solo head spot, of course. His talking style is a bit animated as in sudden punches or elevations of words or phrases. Nothing wrong with this, of course. Just a little interesting and irregular. Lot of laughter weaving through his sentences and pauses. He stays focused on form and sound, frequently "returning" to spotlighting this theme in the course of reading, parsing, analyzing a poem. Of course these 2 items, form and sound, are Yeatsean hallmarks. Lady Gregory described the humming that regularly flowed from Yeats as he composed as a bee buzzing (I've forgotten the exact "buzzing" phrase). He hummed as he wrote, apparently reflecting the way he was experiencing the sense of sound, rhythm, meter in the flow of his lines.

Vendler's way was to create class discussion and simply be a part of the mix (as was Morrissey's). McDonald's way is more of a lecture although he encourages questions and comments and keeps the process informal. Two or three of the men are primary participants with perhaps half of the class doing some participation. The proceedings move lively enough, and a lot of insight emerges.

Maureen and I have dinner at the Glasshouse as the weather is a bit rainy. She reports that her drama class and teacher seemed upset with her announcement that she would not remain to the last day and hence would not participate in the school's presentation of Yeats's "Writing on a Window Pane." Too bad. Maureen feels that the classes have been interesting and insightful in ways that actors approach the process of moving from beginning into the building of a production, and methods used to stimulate and facilitate acting. Maureen has salmon for dinner and I a lamb shank. Then we walk to Hawks Well for a performance by the Brock McGuire band of traditional Irish music—two 1-hour sets. A band that is, they say, widely known in Ireland and America (and probably other lands) for its quality and authenticity. Four instruments, and each performer knows how. Banjo, violin (or is it "fiddle"?), accordion (also called a "camogon"?) and an upright piano.

Rhythmic beat-filled Irish folk. (I wonder what words would exactly describe "Irish" folk music, a sound that is eminently distinctive.) I let my imagination call up as much as I can the senses of generational Irishness in music, thinking even of Sunday's visit to the Megalithic stone sites of Carrowmore, wondering what kind of music they played 6300 years ago in this very land. Thinking how quintessential music is to the human experience and wondering about the first beginning of the tapping toe, or rhythmic hand, or throat-felt voice, or bird-bone flute. Gives a meaning when we describe music as "traditional."

So to bed with Irish sounds inside the head.

Tuesday, August 4

Two excellent lectures and then I meet Maureen for lunch. But we do an alternative to our routine since she has decided to discontinue her drama classes, and my seminar does not begin until 430. We stop at Hargadon's Pub (with which we are becoming familiar). She has tea. I have a pint of you know what.

Then to YMB for the 110 poetry reading. I have generally not described the poetry readings. At this one an older man reads, and then a young woman, Leontia Flynn. Never heard that name before, poet or not. The imagery of her poems is a racing stream of vividness, very imaginative and loaded with vitality. Her speech is hard to understand for me, even though I'm sitting on the front row, but someone sitting further back calls out for louder and she responds by getting louder and slowing down, so I hear the poems. She has a fair amount of rattling-on talk, at typical aside speed-up pace, as spliced-in commentary which is itself worthwhile and charming, at least the connect-the-dots piecing together that I struggle to do. At Keohanes' Bookstore later I order one of her chapbooks (they had had some in stock but now sold out), to pick up Thursday.

We go back to Hargadon's for lunch. Maureen has poached salmon. I have smoked salmon with Irish bread and cream cheese, chopped onion (which I have them add). Our plates contain potato salad and a sort of cole slaw as well. I have a pint (since I have not had one in an hour and a half).

Then to Keohanes' to check on 2 books that have resided on the I'll-have-them-tomorrow waiting list for days, with a revised will-not-arrive for one and the other stays on the I'll-have-it-tomorrow list (although, technically, the word Thursday replaced "tomorrow"). I buy 2 books of poems by Peter Fallon because they appear to address the subject of horses. I decide to buy extra copies to use as gifts to the Hobby's, Saralee and Maureen, partly because its front displays a metal sculpture of Greek antiquity, a hand (child's) holding reins defining a loose delicacy which, at least to a horseman, exhibits a very fine balancing act of control of a power but done with refinement (softness, mastery, confidence). Also I want to see some "horse poems" to see if it can kindle in me a movement into writing horse poems. It seems strange that I haven't written any (with perhaps 2 or 3 exceptions—one recent), in view of my life-long affair with horses and my started-up theme of sculpting horses. We'll see.

Then I go by way of the Glasshouse so I can get to the 430 seminar. A thorough focus on Yeats's children. McDonald mentions that a few years ago his daughter, now a woman, who was singled out in the poem that we read, was present at a Yeats Festival event. In the poem Yeats visits a classroom in the tow of a nun and reminisces about the wash of life though time as children pass into the fray, which he is thinking as a 60-year-old visitor upon the scene. Ends with his famous line: "How can we know the dancer from the dance?" Our focus is, again, on form and sound—the way it's stanza-ed, its variegated exactness of rhyme, the scaling of language, bringing forth characterizations of frame, context, recall.

Afterwards, Maureen and I have a quick bite at the Glasshouse and then to the Methodist Church 830 poetry reading by Michael Longley. He is the husband of Edna Lonlay who lectured earlier in the day with a marvelous presentation. They are academicians from Belfast.

End of Tuesday.

Wednesday, August 5

To Hawks Well where the scheme is 3 lectures instead of 2. The break is after the first 2—one on use of color by Yeats in his poems. I'm not quite recalling what the second one is about, in part because I am writing stuff that seems not to want to get out of my head.

I skip the 3rd lecture in order to get back to Glasshouse to meet Maureen and get on the road for our trip to Mallaghmore, a seaside resort north of Sligo. The trip takes us through Drumcliffe (Drumcliffe Church and Yeats's grave) with mountainous background featuring Ben Bullben (either Ben Bullben or Knockmorea). Martin, one of the locals who has a role in staging the YF, had previously talked with me about the area geology and in fact had procured for me a recently published pamphlet-size book on the geology of the region. He and I had a visit during the break and he provided information about the coastline that we could drive en route to Mallaghmore, and he recommended that we target the Yeats Tavern in Drumcliffe for lunch. We do, and arrive soon. (I find it difficult to adjust to the shortness of distances from town to town, or town to small lightly marked roads that might be our turn-off. In Ireland, 2 miles is something. In Texas, it's not. From the map and distance-thinking that is normal to me, the spot we're seeking should be 15-20 miles, say, and should take some 30 minutes or so, but instead it's 3 miles and takes 8-10 minutes.) We park at the rather large Yeats Tavern, having a "tourist" feeling. Inside it is large and sprawling. We are shown to a table in a crowded room that is 2 or 3 "rooms" away and we begin to make noises for some other table. Then we look at each other and decide to forego Mr. Yeats's tavern. There is nothing poetic about it.

We drive on. Beautiful day and beautiful drive. At a junction or town down the road I get out to inspect a pub and decide no. It is dark, beer-smelly and empty. We do another stop, both going inside. Look at the menu and it has the feel of a sandwich place. We travel on and drive into the seaside edge of the headlands of Mallaghmore, an expansive view of a section of Donegal Bay, looking across the great Atlantic. A harbor with a large man-made brick edifice-wall, accommodating cars to some extent, built like a sea-barrier, or breaker, into the small harbor. Boats and calmness and over across the way, a curving sandy beach. The town consists of buildings lining the land-side of the road that runs along the top of the ridge that rises cliff-like from the harbor. Several pubs toward the end. While Maureen parks I go toward the end to one of the best looking prospects, a pub at the Pier Point Hotel. I encounter as they come out of the pub 2 well-dressed senior citizen men and we strike up a can-you-help-me kind of conversation (a very easy task in Ireland, and it goes on). They are natives and Irish-pleasant. I have come to the right place they say. A little chat about how to drive the headlands (after lunch) for the scenery and pointing out that just there, about 100 yards from where we stand (Maureen has joined us) was the spot where an IRA bomb had taken the lives of Lord Mountbatten, his grandson, Lady Barbourne and a local man, Paul Maxwell, in 1979 (which event I well remember reading about at the time).

The pub's insides are right. The fish chowder is as good as it gets, as is the Guinness (for me, not Maureen). We then do the drive, up and around along the dramatic coastline geology of rock formations and sweeping foamy waves, yielding expansive blue bordered by white splashing at the ocean's encounter with rock and land. Returning in about 40 minutes to the same harbor location we find a place to park and take a lovely stroll along the beach. I collect 4 small rocks that will later take my mind back to this whole spectacle of geology's land and rock and sand meet bay and ocean. The sky and clouds are also present.

Then the drive back to Sligo, stopping for gas fill-up. A quick turn-around at the Glasshouse to head for the racetrack by taxi, about 2 miles on the edge of town. (I had been told at the tourist office that it is easily walkable, about 1 kilometer—but not so. Fortunately we had opted for a taxi.)

The Sligo racetrack is said to be one of the most beautiful racetracks in Ireland, and it must be true. Years ago I paid a number of visits to the track (steeple chasing) at Limerick Junction, near the small place called Cullen, 6 miles out of Tipperary, at the Beachwood House, where Amy and I stayed annually in November with our hosts, Bill and Diana Hobby, for foxhunting. So this trip to the Sligo races is obligatory, since all my many trips to Ireland were always horse-themed.

The landscape is expansive and scenic, soft fields and mountain backdrop. The track is grass, which is the Irish way, a distance (estimating) of a mile plus maybe a little. The covered stand is an open-front structure with concrete steps on which everyone gathers at the beginning of each race to watch from a stand-up position—a good policy. The horses gather at the gate a way down the slope to the left, somewhat within view but a little too far for a meaningful photo. The area in front of the stands is spacious, soft, grassy, green. The finish line (racing direction is clockwise, opposite from the U.S. direction of the course oval) is directly in front of the stands, about 30 yards, with a good view of the field of horses as they complete the last turn on our view to the right, so they can hit the home-stretch stride and culminating which-head-is-in-front pace, as the crowd goes wild. It's always been a thing to note, that is, the urgent cheering, then as quick as crossing a line, the cacophony of yelling closes like a lid, leaving only light and muffled mumbles of groans, or satisfaction noises.

The facilities are all within touching distance, so to speak. The stands, the paddock, the betting stands, the elevated large TV screen, the clubhouse, the entrance and exit gates. The crowd is a gentle mingle of every kind, a sense of an afternoon spirited outing, enjoyed as it's meant to be. Maureen and I can separate with our meanderings without a second thought of where and when we will re-connect. You just take a moment to look about. Maureen bets on 2 races, losing her 2-euro bet on the first but getting a 6-for-2 on the second. So we soon decide to leave while she is 2 euros ahead (and we want to get a quick bite at the Glasshouse then attend the 830 reading at the Methodist Church by 2 poets, one of them Peter Fallon).

Thursday, August 6

This day has the feel of the last day for us at the YF, because it is. Two very good lectures, both by women, with the usual good management of introductions and transitions by Associate Director Maureen Murphy. As we get up from our seats to depart I comment to Bernie (from West Cork whom I've mentioned above, who has become a YF friend and who often sits beside me at the lectures, and I like our chat) that I find it incredible to think of what the Muslim society deprives itself of by excluding women from their ranks. Look at what we just experienced from women!

After lunch together, Maureen and I go separate ways for the afternoon. She wants to see the Isle of Innisfree (quite near the town), the title of a famous Yeats poem. I make my last short walk to Keohanes' where Michael informs me that the waiting-list books will not arrive for me (knowing this is my last day). He offers to send them to me "post-free" but I decline, partly to be gracious, partly because I can probably order them online, and partly because I would not be optimistic that the books would ever be delivered.

I go to my room and pack before the time for my 430, and final, seminar, knowing that there is to be a 630 reception and dinner at the Sligo City Hotel, then an 830 reading at the YMB by student poets —mostly from the workshop of some 14 of us.

The final seminar is good as usual. The reception is a treat by the local people—Chamber of Commerce or equivalent—which is nice. Fine food, wine and visiting. I sit near a woman from New York and we chat. Also a woman from Madrid. She is originally from Ireland, went to Madrid 40 years ago to study Spanish and never left because she met and married. Her husband died 8 years ago. She brought a child and grandchildren to Ireland for this trip, and they are doing other things while she is doing Yeats.

I have been ambivalent about reading my poems at the YMB reading. I ponder the thoughts of "x" number of student-poets one after another and my being a part of that parade, and the attached thought of "who cares?" about all those poems. This "issue" haunts me generally. Finally, however, I decide, well, I'm here, maybe for the only time, so, go ahead.

And I do. I choose "Donkey" and "Humor" to read. There are 20 readers and it takes 2 hours, which is not bad. The room is completely full, probably some 150 people, in the main room of YMB (where other poetry readings have sometimes occurred). I think I read well, am not especially nervous, read slowly and distinctly, and project. So I am pleased. As I exit I receive a few compliments and one woman said the Donkey poem was the best of them all. So I have a small wow in my brain, of course. Next morning at breakfast a man from Pennsylvania ("older" type) stops at my table where I am eating alone and compliments me and noted that he was in the back of the room, has a hearing deficit, and could hear my reading distinctly. I am pleased as I had this as an objective. He liked my poems, said he.

Afterwards, Maureen and I join everyone at Earle's Pub, across the Garavogue about 3 blocks away. Live real Irish music, occasionally having a male vocalist with full authenticity of sound. The pub is very jammed, like Irish pubs sometimes are, locals and poets. Conviviality to the 9's. A kind of celebratory atmosphere (which may be in any case the sense of a good Irish pub evening). Sitting with 2 or 3 fellow poetry workshop students. Barney is a recent Oxford graduate, very attractive, good strong voice, very very bright and talented in my view. His poetry is good. He is about to begin a job in an administrative role at the drama department at Oxford. He's got a wonderful sense of humor. Can do excellent imitations, or mimicking, of accents. For example, a very credible (who am I to know?) Glaswegian accent (which leaves me without the slightest idea of what he says, but it sounds like a Scottish person saying something). He could switch to Cockney. He even tries a Texas accent and does not flunk. I wonder what his future holds. He has been in both of my poetry seminars and in the poetry workshop. I always pay close attention when he speaks or reads. His attitude and participation are very commendable. For me he stands for the high faith I have in our future as human beings.

So, after about an hour, Maureen and I leave Earle's Pub, saying half-heartedly to each other, that perhaps it's good to leave a party when it gets to its full bloom. We have plans to leave to drive to West Cork first thing next morning. That is, the long west side of Ireland, which is not hard to look forward to.

Friday, August 7

I'm thinking of winding down this journal although I have one more week in Ireland, since mostly my purpose has been to capture the Yeats/Sligo experience. We get under way at about 930a. Our projection is Galway, Gort (Coole Park to have a last touch of Yeats), Limerick, Killarney, Bantry, and Ballydehob, one of many small towns along the fingers of peninsulas that fan out along the radiating coast west of Cork, to Maureen's house. Maureen has been in the process of buying, remodeling and opening this house for 2 years (as I have perceived it). Amy and I followed its progress and lack thereof, and had looked forward all of this time to the opportunity to visit, as Maureen most generously extended to us the prospect of doing this when the time arrived. She opened the house in January of this year so obviously Amy did not make it (and Maureen and I have voiced this lament to each other—Maureen and Amy were dear dear friends). This one-day drive from Sligo in the north to West Cork in the far south (along the West of Ireland) is a big anticipation for me. All of my trips to Ireland were mostly to a single area for foxhunting (near Tipperary, Limerick), occasionally with some day trips and especially to Dublin occasionally. This Friday drive will take me through new and exciting towns, landscape and geology.

We meet Maureen's brother, Ross, (whom I know from over the years) at Yeats Tower at about 1p. We get to see the tower where Yeats, his wife and 2 young children, lived for a few years. Challenging to figure out the man and why? Very primitive, one small room per floor, 4 floors and a rooftop place. About 1920. No electricity. No running water, toilets, kitchen facilities like what come later, etc. His wife ("George") must have been really something.

Ross had prepared baskets full of a picnic lunch. We drive on for about 20 minutes to Coole Park, the home of Lady Gregory, where Yeats spent a lot of time, the scene and subject and idea-feed of much of his poetry, the convening grounds (courtesy of Lady Gregory) of many epic Irish writers. A table in a lovely sprawling park area near the "Signature Tree," children and even adults and a dog or two, sunny, cool, a table cloth, a wealth of food and drink, and the pleasure of Ross's thoughtfulness and display of that thing about the Irish that is such a shining generosity in spirit and deed.

Ross is a delight, a barrister by profession (formerly a practicing medical doctor), an inveterate horseman who regularly rides to the hounds, and an education in the classics which fuels very interesting conversation. I ride with Ross from Yeats Tower to Coole Park and we talk a lot about his hunting mare and the young (5-year-old) mare he's bringing along. Both are about ¾ thoroughbred (1/4 draught, or draft, of course), so we talk about how these traits are playing through—performance, toughness of skin, etc. He's thought about the young one for eventing and I'm not sure if he's abandoning that idea. Etc etc. This could go on and on, as I wish at the time.

So we have a one-hour stop-over lunch at Coole Park in just 4 hours. As we depart, Ross leads us around Gort along narrow country roads to avoid single-lane caravans that we would have faced at this rush-hour (rush?) traffic time, and then he waives us on our way. What a great picnic experience!

Maureen is doing all of the driving. I had offered (as I think I said above) to get accredited to be a driver but she kept saying she was ok in her role. She is a good driver and I sit back in the comfort of a sight-seeing passenger, participating in the role of navigator, although our route is not too much of a challenge, especially with Maureen's knowledge.

I'm not sure I want to get much into the topic of the experience of the trip, thinking of ending this journal upon the arrival to Maureen's house. It is fulfillment. Irish towns, the roads, the scenes, how they change, lake towns, mountain views, getting deeper and deeper into pushed-up, crunched-up swirls of sweeping peaks and valleys, with outcroppings of grazing sheep sprinkled up and down and across deep valleys, ravines, hillsides. Narrow roads, twilight slowly beginning to happen, a cell phone call ahead to announce that we would arrive not at 7 but at 9. Three friends are at Maureen's house—Marion (recently widowed on the death of her husband and Maureen's cousin, Jim O'Driscoll), Ean and Patricia McGonigal from Dublin who are staying at Maureen's house along with me. They have lamb stew and wine waiting for us, and we are driving for it. Maureen's family name is O'Driscoll, a prominent and ancient County Cork name. (Amy and I met the late Dr. O'Driscoll and his wife, Maureen's parents, many years ago in Galway having dinner with them at the Ardilaun Hotel on their 50th wedding anniversary. Maureen was born in Cork but grew up in Galway where her father practiced medicine for a lifetime, and where Maureen went to medical school.) I asked Maureen one time if her father missed Cork and she replied: "Every day."

We still had a wee bit of daylight as we got closer to the neighborhood towns with names I did not know at all and could hardly capture the pronunciation of in my head when spoken: Ballydehob, Skibbereen. One I know readily: Baltimore. I marvel at Maureen's driving along the one-lane rows of high hedge-lined overgrowth, sometimes arching almost completely overhead such that we are in a tunnel. The roads are hardly larger than one lane, so when 2 cars meet (always suddenly, it seems, because the roads are hilly/curvy), there is serious adjustment that needs to occur—slowing down to a near stop, pulling into some area to allow the other car to proceed, etc. A sudden crossroad, a turn, motoring on, another turn—a labyrinth that only a rabbit could follow and then only if he knows his briar patch, and road signs haven't been thought of here. Ingeniously, we arrive, about the same time as the sky is kissing the light goodnight. We drive into the driveway of a house that glows inside. Maureen comes home.

Ean greets us as we dismount from the car. Marion and Patricia are inside when Maureen walks in and these three Irish women friends light up and greet and chat like playing 3 radios of talk-shows simultaneously. Maureen has talked in the car about them and their friendships. It is delightful to witness Maureen's gradual rising of coming-home excitement and to be present at the crescendo.

Ean and I take to the deck outside the living room so I can survey the remnant twilight view of Ross Brin Cove and the bay just beyond, the land across the narrow (300 yards?) cove inlet to the right, the castle ruin making a stone monolith in the direct line of sight across the water, the mound of land just beyond (an island, said Ean), another island far out (Cape Clear), small boats riding at anchor in the still water as though sleepily nodding and waiting to be of service.

At the table we have wine and food, adjusting lights until settling on candle light and Willie Nelson twanging his western ballads in the background, the ladies' idea of how to welcome 2 Texans to a Ross Brin Cove abode by the bay. Works for me.

Soon to bed in my assigned room downstairs with a private apartment character. I left the others upstairs appearing to remain in a long distance talkathon for a while longer. Marion to go later to her nearby house and the others to bed later. Maureen had driven all day and must be tired but she is running on special juice.

I sleep well. I can't recall that I've ever not slept well in Ireland.

The ensuing days at Maureen's house with Maureen, Patricia, Ean, Marion, and various comings and goings of friends and encounters at restaurants every evening with glowing ambiance and sightseeing and a special day trip by ferry to Cape Clear and the feel and warmth of the several small Irish towns. Ross comes to town for a restaurant gathering and a night, timed, it seems, to drive me the next day from West Cork through picturesque and interesting Irish land (enhanced by Ross's proclivity for favoring back roads), to the train station in Cork (1 and ½ hours) for my train from Cork to Dublin, for my night in an airport hotel, for my plane ride from Dublin to Houston, for the end of all of the above. So, THE END, almost.

Notes

p. 44   1 Information about the Cruise North Expeditions and its destinations around Hudson Bay can be found at http://www.cruisecritic.com/articles.cfm?ID=1157

   2 You can find the Arctic Circle maps and information at
         http://en.wikipedia.org/wiki/Arctic_Circle
marked to show the line delineating the "tree line" and a line delineating the area within which the temperature does not rise above 10 degrees Celsius (50 degrees Fahrenheit) during the summer . All three concepts are used to define the "Arctic."

P. 48   3 You can find information about the "Inuktitut" writing, and the Inuktitut alphabet, at
         http://en.wikipedia.org/wiki/Inuktitut_syllabics.

p. 60   4 This journal was written contemporaneously on the journey in longhand, then typed with virtually no editing, revisions or additions. To appease the urge to add information or comment at the time of typing, this is done in footnotes. To me it seemed important for this account to have on-site impressions, fresh, written on-the-fly, for better or worse. It will not capture everything, but only what I was able to write down when a writing window was open. It would be a different story if reported by another person, of course, but this is how it unfolded to me. I decided against commenting on the people in the group, whom I enjoyed very much. Of course, the photos are spliced in at the time of typing.

p. 73   5 Lecture by Professor Farrell: Natural History of Amazon Animals and Plants—What are we seeing?

p. 75   6 Lecture by Professor Farrell: What are we hearing? The Acoustic biology of the Amazon Animals

p. 85   7 Lecture by Professor Farrell: Untold Diversity: Documenting Species.

p. 89   8 Lecture by Professor Farrell: Conservating the Future.

p. 91   9 Lecture by Professor Farrell: Recordings from the trip and Amazon Archeology

p. 109   10 This journal was written in longhand "on the fly" almost entirely, when I could catch moments for writing, which was hard to do. More than a year later (November, '10) I am typing it up. To maintain a freshness and spontaneity, I have refrained from revising/correcting (except I have checked spelling and looked up names of places that I could not insert from the top of my head at writing time). So, some errors are present. An objective in this journal is to present it the way it unfolded to me, at the time of unfolding. Footnotes and photos are added at the time of typing.

p. 112   11 From Wikipedia: Yeats's mother, Susan May Pollesfen, came from a wealthy Anglo-Irish family in County Sligo who owned a prosperous milling and shipping business. Soon after William's birth the family relocated to Sligo to stay with her extended family, and the young poet came to think of the area as his childhood and spiritual home. Its landscape became, over time, both literally and symbolically, his "country of the heart". The Butler Yeats family were highly artistic; his brother Jack went on to be a highly regarded painter, while his sisters Elizabeth and Susan Mary—known to family and friends as Lollie and Lily—became involved in the Arts and Crafts movement.

p. 116   12 My decision is not to attempt literary criticism in this journal except for occasional general words. Such an attempt involves time and care in writing that would get in the way of a fast-pace travel journal. The circumstances and process require a fast pace, as indicated in note 4.

p. 117   13 I note at this time of typing (November, '10) that Sinead has just been awarded a £5,000 Irish Times poetry prize. She has excellent internet presence if you google, and among other things she is praised for her reading skills (!).

www.ingramcontent.com/pod-product-compliance
Lightning Source LLC
Chambersburg PA
CBHW050502110426
42742CB00018B/3339